"MY PRAYER IS THAT YOU WILL FIND SOMETHING HERE TO WARM
YOUR HEART, FEED YOUR SPIRIT, AND NOURISH YOUR SOUL.
DRINK, MY SISTERS."

—Jacqueline Jakes, from the Introduction

PRAISE FOR THE INSPIRING WISDOM
OF JACQUELINE JAKES

"Offers devotional wisdom. . . . Like most great men and women of God, her ministry is evolving from her misery. . . . her testimony in book form [is] a way for the world to experience her triumphant victory."　　　*—Dallas Examiner*

"SISTER WIT offers a daily dose of encouragement that comforts the soul and the spirit . . . [and] will push readers to extend their limits, challenge their minds, and increase their faith."　　　　　*—Upscale*

"Jakes reaches out to every woman. She has 'unstitched the words of this book from the cloth of my soul.' It is a fine, richly textured garment that will comfort readers' hearts."　　　　　*—Charisma*

"Jacqueline Jakes earned a measure of wisdom after her ordeal, but she has managed to transcend her problems, while offering readers encouragement through the words of the Bible."　　　*—Black Images Book Review Magazine*

"Filled with so much insight, courage, and inspiration that it will leave you shaking your head in agreement with the profound insights so simply yet accurately expressed."　　　　　*—MyShelf.Com*

"With personal revelations as well as uplifting quotations . . . Jacqueline reminds us that God is mindful of you, He is with you, He is where medicine cannot reach, He is where sound cannot travel, where darkness is the deepest, and where pain is the most extreme."　　　　　*—Good News Gazette*

D0424146

SISTER WIT

Devotions for Women

JACQUELINE JAKES

Foreword by
T. D. JAKES

WARNER
Faith

A Division of AOL Time Warner Book Group

Unless otherwise noted Scriptures are taken from the HOLY BIBLE: NEW INTERNATIONAL VERSION®. Copyright © 1973, 1978, 1984 by International Bible Society. Used by permission of Zondervan Publishing House. All rights reserved.

W WARNER *Faith* A Division of AOL Time Warner Book Group

Scriptures noted KJV are taken from the King James Version of the Bible.

Visit our Website at www.twbookmark.com

Printed in the United States of America
Originally published in hardcover by Warner Faith
First Warner Faith Trade Printing: January 2004
10 9 8 7 6 5 4 3 2 1

Hardcover ISBN: 0-446-52972-9
Paperback ISBN: 0-446-69048-1
LCCN: 2001098348

Book Design by Charles Sutherland
Cover Designer Claire Brown
Photo Credit: JOHNER/Photonica

This book is dedicated to the memory of my mother, Odith P. Jakes, without whom I would never have had a classical foundation.

And to my daughter, Kelly, who was my night-light during a decade of darkness. You are the love of my life. I adore you.

Lastly, this book is dedicated to all women who struggle with an illness or who battle any terror. I pray that God will wash you in miracles and give you total well-being for all your life.

CONTENTS

Virtues   125

Encouragement   187

Acknowledgments

There would be no *Sister Wit* without Bishop T. D. Jakes. It was he who asked me to share my testimony with others. From his embryonic idea developed the idea of a book to share with other women—a devotional containing the wisdom of my unique experience and the challenges of this life. Thus *Sister Wit* was born. Thank you, my precious baby brother—thank you, my stellar Bishop.

Cheryl L. Thomas, had you not stood by with your spirit of excellence, organizing, typing, retyping, and saving this manuscript and simply doing whatever you were asked to do to help me get this book finished, I don't know what I would have done.

Rolf Zettersten, thank you for the incredible insight and direction for this book.

Leslie Peterson, your sharp editor's pencil and your ability to identify with me uniquely made this a pleasurable experience. Thank you for being a delight to work with.

Kelly, your comments and applause helped to strengthen me and to keep me on track and to believe in myself. You are an exceptional daughter!

Marci Russell and Jane Darrisaw, thanks for every time you cheered with me throughout each step of the book publishing process. Thank you for believing in me.

Ernest Jakes Jr., Margaret, Sherry, Sister Mays, Laurena, Brenda, DeLaunda, and all the many people everywhere who prayed for me and cheered me along to completion—thank you from my heart.

Tom Winters, you and Debby are the greatest. Thank you for everything.

Foreword

And the woman conceived, and bare a son: and when she saw him that he was a goodly child, she hid him three months. And when she could not longer hide him, she took for him an ark of bulrushes, and daubed it with slime and with pitch, and put the child therein; and she laid it in the flags by the river's brink. And his sister stood afar off, to wit what would be done to him.

Exodus 2:2-4 KJV

It has been a long watch from across the room—a watch of forty-plus years for my sister. I have gone to the palace and she has stood in the courts, watching from the gates and encouraging as she has done all of my life. It seems only yesterday that I sat on the steps of our very modest home dressed in short pants with the stinging whelps of Momma's switch still tartly staining my pride as I had once again managed to get myself in the incorrigible dilemmas of childhood pranks. My sister's bright eyes and deep penetrating gaze observed my punishment. She comforted my whimpers when the discipline was too much for me to bear.

I can only wonder what rush of wind has swept away the years between those long ago days to this present moment. All I know is that when the wind slowed its gusting my hair resembled the glistening snow-capped mountains of a West Virginia Christmas card. But to my surprise, after a lovely wife and five children of my own, my sister was still standing by me, watching me sail down the muddy rivers of life covered in bull rushes and relentlessly pursuing my dreams. These were the dreams that could only be completed if she watched like a spotter in a gym to make sure that the weight of life's pressure did not dement the magnitude of God's calling on my life.

Well, it has certainly been a fast-paced, eventful, and sometimes breath-taking trip. Many things have changed—except the woman gazing across the room at me. My sister is filled with wit and wisdom. Her thought-provoking perspectives on life, love, and the many pitfalls in between are filled with a tremendous legacy passed to us from our parents, who before expiring hurled us into the wind of life with the force of champions. Their strength still resounds in all of their children. Even if nothing but an accounting of my sister's observations while watching over me, this book would still be inspirational enough to prepare the hearts of the thoughtful women who mentor, marry, minister, or muster courage in the midst of storms.

My sister far excels a voyeur whose only claim is to have recorded the trappings of thought that are threaded throughout this book. No. She on her own rights has had quite an experience in the courts of life: raising a child, surviving perils, fighting the brain tumor that finally gave way to her relentless determination to live. She has, like a little girl collecting seashells, gathered pearls of wisdom.

Now she is ready to be presented her pearls. Her tiara is the thorny crown that is reserved only for those who have suffered hardships, endured storms, and survived predicaments too horrendous to be articulated. Her soul, like those of all who have had a real adventure, has become the rose that brightens the lives of us all. Her thorny path may usher tears to stream down our face. But her resiliency will motivate the disadvantaged to rise from the ashes of mediocrity and fulfill their dreams.

I cannot give her to you. She is too precious to be given away. But for the next few days I will allow you to gaze at the wisdom that has been the fodder we have used to survive the vicissitudes of life. Today she has been garlanded with grace and seasoned with prayer. She now emerges from her shadowed posture, where in times past she has avoided the glaring light of notoriety, to unveil the wit that has tailored her soul and balanced my judgment all of these years we have spent together here in the Egypt of life in the house of Pharaoh.

T. D. Jakes

INTRODUCTION

Every woman has a story to tell. You, dear reader, are most likely not a Coretta Scott King, who has faced suffering and the loss of a spouse and who has lived a life on public display. And more than likely you are not a Helen Keller, who triumphed over her every limitation to become a household name—a woman who overcame seemingly insurmountable odds. Instead, you're probably like myself, an ordinary woman who faced extraordinary circumstances and survived intact. Survived stronger and wiser. Survived to tell you that you too can come out of whatever circumstance you are facing—better, not bitter.

No, you don't need to be famous to have some special claim on overcoming affliction. Simply passing through this earth seems to be enough. We live in a world fraught with the unexpected and laced with the unknown. What do we do when the gnarled fingers of terrifying experiences knock at our door? Facing challenges with peace, love, and even joy is the order of the day. And depending on God.

It was my faith in God that held my falling soul together

throughout an eight-hour brain surgery. It was my total dependence on Him that got me through the aftermath—that allowed me to be carried by Him through the unexplored and never-before-seen places and into recovery. My faith in God is what brought me to where I am today.

Sister Wit contains the wisdom I collected along that journey. Like most wisdom, it was born in the furnace of affliction. So many of us are women bound together in tribulation. We have seen loss, buried our parents, sometimes even our children. So many of our bodies have been invaded and redesigned by the surgeon's knife. The twenty-first-century woman is widowed, divorced, single, remarried with a blended family. She is living with illness and addiction. She is abused. She is unemployed or underemployed. She is lonely. She is you. She is me.

Am I discouraged? Absolutely not! It is hard to discourage a woman who has gone to sleep before a man with a scalpel at her head. At twenty-nine years of age, my mind was not astute enough, nor imaginative enough to begin to know what the next nearly ten years of my life would be. You see, I was told about the surgery. I was told I could be paralyzed on one side of my body. I was told that if the tumor was cancerous I would need radiation. I was told that very possibly my peripheral vision would be gone—and it is. They said they would shave my hair—they did. They told me they would put hot dye in the veins and arteries of my head for the arteriogram—and it was very hot. They said that if the arteriogram didn't show what they wanted to see, I could not leave the hospital; it would mean emergency brain surgery. I left the hospital . . . eleven days later.

Everything that happened after the surgery I had to figure out by myself. No one prepared me for the fight of my life. Nothing gave me any inclination that normalcy would become one of the most desirable gifts I would ever ask of God. I did not know I was entering a strange place where the soul and the spirit disconnect, where you are lost and groping to connect the altered places together again—a place where you do not feel like or have the ability to recognize yourself. A place no one can get you out of. Except God.

I went to hell emotionally, but God never left me. As David said, "If I make my bed in hell, behold, thou art there" (Ps. 139:8 KJV). In that place where medicine could not reach and people could not travel, God stood with me and held me through the nights and rocked me during the days. For years. Until one glad morning, of which I do not know the day nor the hour, He rocked me until He rocked me out. Out into health. Out into the light. Out into normalcy. Out into total well-being.

Right now you may be facing dark nights, as I once did. If so, I have jotted down a few writings to encourage you—to inspire and refresh you and to help usher you into the dawning of your new day. I encourage you to let the Lord Jesus Christ, who is the Light of my world, shine His glory onto your situation and into your life. His presence will be medicine for your soul. When you have nothing to lose, when all is gone, try Jesus. Better yet, before you have lost everything, before all is gone, call on Jesus. He is a sure choice.

I urge you to stand on God's Word. During my time of struggle, I drank in His Word. I ate it. I slept with it, surrounded every room in my house with it. I memorized it, sang it, and whispered its words to myself. Therefore I know what I'm talking about when I assure you that God's Word is a sure and solid foundation on which to anchor your hopeful soul. In a severe test, it is all you will have the strength to cling to.

A very dear friend of mine, after reading the preceding passages, said, "I knew you had brain surgery, but you never told me you went through all of that. You don't look as if you suffered like that." I love that comment. It let's me know that I've survived—that the God I depend so greatly on has gotten me through something I couldn't have gotten through on my own. That His love conquers all. And it gives me the confidence to tell you He will do exactly the same for you, whatever your situation—big or small.

Sister Wit is written to help you celebrate, heal, and re-create the life God has given you to live. For that cause, I have unstitched the words of this book from the cloth of my soul. My prayer is that you will find something to warm your heart, feed your spirit, and nourish your soul. Drink, my sisters.

INSPIRATION

The Magic of Wonder

And they were calling to one another: "Holy, holy, holy is the LORD Almighty; the whole earth is full of his glory."

ISAIAH 6:3

Wonder is music heard in the heart.

ROSEMARY DOBSON

Today is no ordinary day. Every day we rise, we have the opportunity to witness the extraordinary. The very atmosphere teems with the presence of God. The sun's warm, golden rays shine into our windows. God claps His hands over this planet and we watch Him paint His love in living color, lavishly splashing radiant beauty onto the skies, abundantly covering the hills, the fields, the flowers and leaves.

Without words, each day we experience the rhythmic throb of life. You and I, the very dust of the earth, watch as heavenly magic visits us with atmospheric drama. We may enjoy the warm luster of a colored rainbow or walk over buried treasures of coal, oil, minerals. Invisible gifts roar past us without our noticing—

electricity and sound waves. The force of the wind is a full symphony orchestra in concert. And bubbling, white clouds tower high into the sky while the surprise of a brilliant sunset silently exhibits masterpieces of the universe. All designed to draw our attention away from the details of our day.

Nature cannot hide the awe of God; rather, it has been hired to render the service of revealing those divine gifts strewn throughout the earth and flung under open heavens and freely given for you and me to enjoy. As we lay our heads down to sleep under the black face of the night sky while twinkling, shimmering stars light a path of glory, remember: the brilliance of God's footprints are found everywhere.

Give praise to the Creator!

What about the Other Woman?

Each of you should look not only to your own interests, but also to the interests of others.

PHILIPPIANS 2:4

A candle loses nothing by lighting another candle.

ERIN MAJORS

It's easy for us to move through this life oblivious to each other and to the people we encounter day by day. We become so preoccupied with responsibilities, commitments, and relationships that we do not notice the lady next door. The lady in church. The woman at our job.

Whether we know it or not, we are all responsible for one another. The twenty-first century is long on information and short on communication. We can acquire information from almost anyplace and about anything and yet we do not know the state of our neighbor, our church sister, or our female relatives.

How rare and pleasant it is when someone stops by to check to see how our day is going, to inquire about a recent event in our life, or simply to take a moment to show interest in what is happening in our world and allow us a brief interlude of sharing. Cultivating the habit of concerning ourselves with one another is worth the sacrifice and yields a wholesome and luscious harvest of results that nurture our spirit and nourish our soul.

A card in the mail gives hope to someone who needs encouragement. A phone call helps a friend feel cared for or thought about. A word of encouragement brightens a day. In this day when hardly anyone prepares a home-cooked meal, an invitation for an evening of talking, laughing, sharing, and breaking bread together is a delightful and refreshing treat.

Remembering to check on the other woman is just one simple way to make your world a brighter and sweeter place to live.

STAY IN LOVE

Jesus replied: "Love the Lord your God with all your heart and with all your soul and with all your mind." This is the first and greatest commandment. And the second is like it: "Love your neighbor as yourself."

MATTHEW 22:37-39

Love is life and if you miss love, you miss life.

LEO BUSCAGLIA

When it comes right down to it, we don't have much choice in the matter. We are told to do everything in love. We are to speak the truth in love. We are to minister in love. We are to give in love. We don't have an option.

Why do the Scriptures tell us over and over that we must abide in love? Because love is the foundation of Christ's kingdom. Jesus didn't beat around the bush on this one. He specifically detailed to us the two greatest commandments that sum up the totality of God's message, both of which deal with love. You couldn't be much clearer than that. He made it clear to his disciples and to us how we are expected to live.

Love is the ruler we use to measure our walk with Christ. No matter the intensity of the anointing, the conviction in the voice, the gleam in the eye, or any other outward sign, the final gauge God uses to determine the quality of our relationship is love. Love must be evident and intrinsically woven throughout every area of our lives. It cannot be pretended. It cannot be done halfway. Love is all or nothing.

Do as Christ commanded. Allow love to permeate you. Allow it to take the shape of the cross in your life—love horizontally toward your neighbor and love vertically toward God.

Spiritual Rituals

Put on the new man, which is renewed in knowledge after the image of him that created him.

COLOSSIANS 3:10 (KJV)

Learn to get in touch with the silence within yourself. There's no need to go to India or somewhere else to find peace. You will find it in your room, your garden, or even your bathroom.

ELISABETH KÜBLER-ROSS

It is so easy for us to find or make excuses for not praising God. However, I recently incorporated a ritual into my life that you might want to try.

All of us know about morning devotions—that time when we deliberately set aside a moment to commune with God and read His Word. But often, because we're late for work or school or have an unexpected chore, we find ourselves passing over the chance to do so. My solution is this: why not praise and commune with God in the morning while doing the things you do every morning? Like taking your shower. Or riding your exercise bike. Or walking the dog. Even while making the coffee! During these times you have the perfect opportunity to praise and thank God for His blessings.

I always lotion my entire body; it is an unbreakable habit. So each morning I take this time to worship. As I moisturize my face, I anoint it to shine with the light of the Lord. Likewise, for my lips to utter His words, for my eyes to see what He would share with me this day, and for my ears to hear His voice. As I lotion my body, I anoint my legs to walk in places of peace and my feet to carry good tidings wherever I go. For my arms to provide healing embraces and for healing virtue to slip through my hands and fingers out to others throughout the day. By the time I am ready to dress I feel I have put on not only the whole armor of God, but the Lord Himself.

Why not make up your own daily spiritual rituals. When you greet the day with your routine, you can experience new life and fellowship with the Lord. And you will notice how differently you feel as you leave your home having connected with Him who is our Life, Light, and Leader.

Special to God

I will praise thee; for I am fearfully and wonderfully made: marvellous are thy works; and that my soul knoweth right well.

PSALM 139:14 (KJV)

When the Stars threw down their spears, / And watered heaven with their tears, / Did he smile his work to see? / Did he who made the Lamb make thee?

WILLIAM BLAKE

Big cities can be fun. Walk down their huge sidewalks, in the shadow of buildings that tower far into the sky, and you will undoubtedly pass by many people who look different, sound different, and dress differently from yourself. It is wonderful to see others who have the same skin color as you but perhaps not the same language, or who are dissimilar in other ways. Watch their body language and mannerisms. Smell their foods. Listen to their accents, to exotic-sounding words that flow like a bubbling brook on a summer walk through the woods.

Being different is certainly not bad. Being different is unique. It means choice, surprise, and infinite variety. It means the chance to experience differences in a positive way and to learn new things. It means you can be sure there is no one in the world exactly like you—you are unique and special!

Never copy anyone else's style. Show us who you are. We wonder who would show through if you didn't try to mimic the woman on that TV show or the lady in your church or your coworker. It's fine to appreciate others and to try and incorporate their qualities into your own self. But that is not an excuse to try and be someone you are not and were never meant to be. Being you is something only you can do. You are unlike any other creation God has made. You have been set apart. You have a mark of distinction.

Each of us displays the genius of God. Let our differences be a reminder that we are custom-designed masterpieces.

POTPOURRI

May the God who gives endurance and encouragement give you a spirit of unity among yourselves as you follow Christ Jesus.

ROMANS 15:5

Liberty, when it begins to take root, is a plant of rapid growth.

GEORGE WASHINGTON

Our great country, the melting pot of the universe, is made up of so many beautiful races and colors and ethnic backgrounds. Diversity is wonderful. Here, you and I have the opportunity to become connoisseurs of others' cultures—to learn to appreciate the assorted elements of our rainbow society. It is an exciting blessing.

I realize that some people believe in separatism and lament the influx of so many cultures into our society. However, the Scriptures teach us to love one another. And in order for us to love one another, we must seek to understand, appreciate, and sometimes emulate each other.

Dwelling in unity does not mean dwelling with only those that look or dress like you or that eat the same cuisine. Dwelling in unity means to abide with people of contrasting looks, varied languages, and diverse customs. Adopt into your own life those things from various cultures that fascinate you. Go see foreign movies that depict life from other parts of the world. Go out to new restaurants and sample foods that have come to us from the other side of the globe. Do you like a particular style or type of clothing from another culture? Go out and buy it! It is a privilege to be able to adopt into our lifestyles customs and physical representations from others that titillate our fancy or strike our interest.

Just because other human beings are different from you doesn't mean they're wrong. Pray to the Father for the spirit of unity. His love will bind us together and make us one.

Too much similarity is boring!

People of the Past

Rise in the presence of the aged, show respect for the elderly and revere your God. I am the Lord.

LEVITICUS 19:32

How far you go in life depends on your being tender with the young, compassionate with the aged, sympathetic with the striving, and tolerant of the weak and strong. Because someday in your life you will have been all of these.

GEORGE WASHINGTON CARVER

I wish I had known that I stood in the presence of greatness, but I was a child and did not know. And now I have only soft and hazy memories of my great-grandmother—a slave. Yes, I am a descendant of slaves. I saw my grandmother, touched her, and kissed her rough, dark cheek. But my fear of her past, regardless of her quiet demeanor as she sat in her rocking chair in her meticulously clean home, frightened me, and so I did not speak much with her. A slave—a real-life slave. How strange that seemed to my young mind.

Today, I am so proud of my great-grandmother. How much I

wish I had been aware enough then to know what I know today and to tell her so. Instead, on the day I am now remembering, I obeyed my parents and went outside to our car—driven hundreds of miles to her home for our summer vacation—got my little saxophone out of its case, and began to play for her. The music was the only communion between us.

What great people are around you today? Are you aware of the elderly—those people who struggled through the Depression, who lived through the wars, who survived the Holocaust? Are they in your midst? If so, rise and show respect, and inquire of them. Learn from them. They have so much wisdom to impart to you, so much advice, so many stories to tell. Would you not want your own descendants to benefit from your own wisdom when you grow old?

It is so important to give our attention to our elders. They have much to share with us that we need to know.

Magic in the Air

And be ye kind one to another, tenderhearted, forgiving one another, even as God for Christ's sake hath forgiven you.

EPHESIANS 4:32

I will never understand all the good that a simple smile can accomplish.

MOTHER TERESA

Before you can be the recipient of a gift, or anything, you must open your hand, your mind, your heart. You'll notice I didn't say mouth. But there is a way to do all the above without saying even a word. The simplest way to bestow a blessing, shed light, and dispense joy each and every day is . . . to smile.

When you gift someone with a smile you deliver silent, warm sunshine into their life. Without a word, you have let them know you esteem them; you have affirmed their existence and encouraged them. The simplest way to unlock someone is by smiling at them. And smiles are like yawns—they're contagious. The person you smiled at will in turn smile at someone else. And they'll smile at someone else. And pretty soon everyone around you will be smiling.

Many, many years ago, I sat in my car stuck in miles of traffic in downtown Washington, D.C. As we inched along I happened to glance over to another lane, just in time to receive one of the sweetest smiles that I can remember. I'll never know who that person was, and she will never know how much she impacted my day and my life. Years later, she is still able to bring a smile to my own face.

Smiles are the fragrance of a breeze rinsed in rose petals. They can brighten a day, lighten a load, distract gloom, and renew hope.

Find someone to smile at. Anyone. Every day. Just smile.

Sister to Brother,
Sister to Sister

Honour thy father and thy mother: that thy days may be long upon the land which the LORD thy God giveth thee.

EXODUS 20:12 (KJV)

Nobody has ever measured, not even poets, how much the heart can hold.

ZELDA FITZGERALD

Perhaps you are fortunate enough to have a sibling who shares your heritage, history, DNA, values, and beliefs. It is a treasure to have those people in your life to whom you are emotionally connected without even having to work at it.

It was this sort of connection that helped me understand what my baby brother was feeling as he put my oldest brother and me, along with Momma and a nurse, onto a Lear jet one sunny summer day. We were headed to yet another hospital so Momma could have tests run (that would later result in two surgeries).

The pained look on my brother's face as we boarded the tiny plane said it all. He was watching his entire history, the people who shared his past, and the mother he treasured leave him. It was a hard thing to do.

Such is the bond between siblings. And such should be the bond among the children of God. We are all of the same blood—the blood of Christ—and we should treat each other accordingly.

While we walk out our days on this earth, you and I have the opportunity to be a blessing to one another. As members of the family of God, we have the same Father, and He expects us to bind together—to be supportive and loyal to one another. There is a wonderful diversity of brothers and sisters in the body of Christ. It is a privilege to be a part of such an incredibly large and divine unit. What a joy to share our blessings, our gifts, our love, our knowledge, and our strength and courage with one another. We are bound together, speaking the same language. We understand our roots, our creation, and we have an expectation of the same glorious future.

Our culture is rich because we know Jesus, our elder brother, is the answer to every question and our kingdom operates by His love. What a sweet relief and comfort to be part of this eternal empire.

YOU HAVE MAIL!

The heavens declare the glory of God; and the firmament sheweth his handywork.

PSALM 19:1 (KJV)

All I have seen teaches me to trust the creator for all I have not seen.

RALPH WALDO EMERSON

Don't you love going to the mailbox—physical or e-mail—and finding a letter from a dear friend? Opening up a note and seeing who has corresponded with us makes us feel good and lets us know someone cares about us. It brightens our day. It adds *oomph* to our step and a glint to our eye.

But what about letters from God? What of the missives He sends us through nature? The gleaming dawn of a new day . . . The delicious scent of blossoms in the air . . . The quiet trilling of a nightingale . . .

Not many of us have taken the time to stop, look, and listen to the many messages of affection God sends us each day. He longs to show us just how much He cares, and so He reaches out and touches us with the beauty of nature. With each season comes a different expression of communication from Him—a quiet, moonlit snowfall, a daisy-spangled meadow, the rainbow after a spring storm. All these announcements demonstrate to the world how much He loves us. And it gives us the chance to behold the reflection of Him through the beauty that abounds throughout this earth.

Take the time to notice God's love for you. Take a morning walk or an evening stroll and listen to Him proclaim His abiding faithfulness. Don't fail to read the love letters He sends you each day through His incomparable creation.

Look! You have heavenly mail waiting for you!

JUMPING FOR JOY

My soul glorifies the Lord and my spirit rejoices in God my Savior.

LUKE 1:46-47

Today, whatever may annoy, the word for me is joy, just simple joy.

JOHN KENDRICK BANGS

There ought to be times in your life that for no reason you find yourself jumping for joy. As the old song goes, "Have you ever woke up singing and praising God?" These are the times when your spirit knows what your mind has not gotten an e-mail about. When you experience joy without evidence, look out! Something wonderful is on the way to you.

Unexplained joy is praise in the city of your soul. When you feel good from the center of your body to the outer limits, your innermost being is celebrating a victory that your eyes haven't seen and your ears haven't heard.

Continually, throughout the Scriptures we are admonished to

rejoice in the Lord. Rejoice in His name. Rejoice in His goodness, His mercy, and His kindness. When your spirit rejoices, God is giving you a preview of a coming attraction. He is allowing the spirit within you to unveil a future event to you.

Now, we as humans are triune beings; we are made up of mind, body, and spirit. We commune with God in our spirit—it is where, when God wishes to speak with us, His heavenly information comes first. Your spirit knows secrets that are to come, that your mind does not yet understand. Your body is the last to get the news.

Pay attention the next time you get that glorious spiritual excitement that causes you to rejoice. Know that as Dr. Oral Roberts so often says, "Something good is going to happen to you!"

"Again, I say rejoice!" (Phil. 4:4 KJV).

HEALING WORDS

Pleasant words are a honeycomb, sweet to the soul and heal-ing to the bones.

PROVERBS 16:24

To love oneself is the beginning of a lifelong romance.

OSCAR WILDE

It is quite acceptable to give gifts to one another in our culture. We give each other toys, cards, love, and compliments. But it is quite uncommon to lavish gifts upon ourselves. In fact, in today's society it is frowned upon and considered selfish to esteem or cele-brate oneself. How odd that we would without hesitation bless and encourage another individual, yet never contemplate using the same attitude to bless ourselves! I suppose the fear of becoming or being considered self-centered overshadows reason. Scriptures tell us that David encouraged himself. Jacob strengthened himself on his deathbed in order to speak blessings to his sons. Mary the moth-er of Jesus acknowledged that God had seen her low estate and all generations would call her blessed (Luke 1:46-48).

Don't wait until the next time you feel low or discouraged to speak wholeness to yourself. Form a daily habit of giving yourself the gift of kind words—words that heal and bless. Indeed, it is the use of your tongue that shapes your very existence. Therefore, shun every distressing word. Once it's apparent to you how powerful words are, you will flee from speaking such idiomatic expressions as "I am sick of . . ." or "That gives me a pain in the neck" or "So-and-so gets on my nerves!" Today, begin to build the walls of your life with words that will lend to your total well-being. Speak only those things you wish to see reflected in your body, your mind, your health, and your home.

"The tongue has the power of life and death" (Prov. 18:21). Remember to speak life!

It's Happening Now!

———— ⌘ ————

Peter followed him out of the prison, but he had no idea that what the angel was doing was really happening; he thought he was seeing a vision. Peter knocked at the outer entrance, and a servant girl named Rhoda came to answer the door. When she recognized Peter's voice, she was so overjoyed she ran back without opening it and exclaimed, "Peter is at the door!" "You're out of your mind," they told her. When she kept insisting that it was so, they said, "It must be his angel." But Peter kept on knocking, and when they opened the door and saw him, they were astonished.

ACTS 12:9-16

Questions are never indiscreet. Answers sometimes are.

OSCAR WILDE

You would not think a person could spend a great portion of time in prayer on a specific request or special petition and then, when what they're looking for actually arrives, be so astonished they fail to recognize their prayer has been answered. But that is exactly what is written about in the Book of Acts. It is, however, not a story relevant only to biblical days. Today, many of us have had the same response to answered prayer.

Have you ever immersed yourself in prayer for so long and so intensely that when the answer arrived, you stood in disbelief and questioned God as to what was happening in your life? It is hard to fathom that kind of blindness, but the reality is your circumstances can leave you so conditioned that it may take a while for you to see correctly. Lest you think this does not apply to you, look around and make certain that the very thing you have asked God for is not standing somewhere in your life knocking and waiting for you to acknowledge your own answered prayer.

Some friends once shared with me about a "faith box" they used when they wanted something from God. In the faith box they put one, two, or three small items to remind them of what they were asking God. The box was left in an open and obvious place to remind them of their request before the Lord. They shared with me that this box kept them focused. When the answer arrived, they simply packed the box with other requests and moved in a new prayer direction.

I tried the prayer box while working in an undesirable position. I kept the box on my desk with a few personal items inside. Sure enough, after a long while, I received a phone call offering me my dream job. I simply put my remaining personal items into the box, completed the necessary paperwork, and was ready to go! There was no confusion about what was happening. I had been looking for this answer, had kept the vision before me, and was now receiving what I had sought from God.

If you've been praying for a new home, a new apartment, a new job, or whatever, you may want to try a faith box. Pack it with a few things and place it so that it is in your constant view while you continue to pray and seek God for your answer. When you get your answer, you will know that "It's happening now!"

Girlfriend, You Are a
Friend of the King!

I no longer call you servants, because a servant does not know his master's business. Instead, I have called you friends, for everything that I learned from my Father I have made known to you.

JOHN 15:15

Friend: the finest word in any language.

TALBOT JENNINGS

If you know anything about friendship, you recognize it as a precious and rare commodity. Friendship is the warmth of a cheery fire on a crisp autumn day; it shimmers in the hearts of those who offer and receive it. Good friends are beautifully and deeply connected. They know how to bring hope where there is despair and how to soothe with love and laughter and consolation that chases away sorrow. Friends make our lives flow more smoothly, like the swirling cool waters of a clear, hidden stream. They rejuvenate us.

It is well worth every effort to cultivate our specialness to one another. When we do so, we realize what a privilege friendship is, to be guarded and cherished.

So it is with our heavenly Father. We are friends of the King. He is our unseen companion, our divine support system, and our celestial confidant. Our earthly friendships are only shadows of the heavenly covenant of friendship that binds and strengthens us. In our Lord, we have someone to love and trust who will visit us for long, intimate talks and provide us with wise counsel and soul-shaking inspiration. At any time day or night, we can call Him, talk with Him, and share our most intimate secrets and concerns. The friendship we have with the King is trustworthy. He cares about what concerns us. Because He is not a fair-weather friend, He will stay with us through our dark days. And when life brings some morsel too precious, too divine, and too exhilarating to initially share with another, it is Christ who stands with us in rejoicing.

As you celebrate your friends with gifts and cards and other expressions of endearment, remember to celebrate too your greatest Friend, with praise and adoration and worship. It is no small thing to be a friend of the King.

The Fragrance of Beauty

All thy garments smell of myrrh, and aloes, and cassia, out of the ivory palaces, whereby they have made thee glad.

PSALM 45:8

Give beauty back, beauty, beauty, beauty, back to God, beauty's self and beauty's giver.

GERARD MANLEY HOPKINS

This earth is filled with many hidden treasures. Smell is one of them. A simple stroll through a flower-filled park or woods, where blossoms fill the air with their scent, can be a delightful experience. What we smell through our noses affects us profoundly—affects even our behavior.

Today we have many mood enhancers. Aromatherapy is big business. We wish to pleasure our emotions and each other through smell. We have discovered that what we sniff on the outside affects us inwardly. So we pay to have soaps, creams, mists, incense, and candles with which to fill our homes and workplaces. We seek to control our environment through smell.

But what of the scent of the soul? Do we not, as the soft flowers of a field, give off our own personal perfume? Scripture tells us to put on the Lord Jesus Christ. I think one reason is so that we may smell of Him. Not only are we washed by Him, but He perfumes us with His presence and we are made beautiful. By wearing Him, we refuse to wear the aroma of arrogance or cologne of poor character. Those are not scents we wish to fan into the nostrils of those we encounter during each day!

So before you leave your home this morning, mist yourself in His presence through prayer, psalm, song, or praise. It is your level of devotion to Him that will determine the silent scent of your soul.

The Right Side of Forty: Forever Young

———— ✦ ————

You, however, will go to your fathers in peace and be buried at a good old age.

GENESIS 15:15

How old would you be if you didn't know how old you was?

SATCHEL PAIGE

The most incredible thing happened to me when I turned forty—life became almost immediately, immensely better! Like most ladies, I had been programmed to believe that life beyond forty was going to be a downhill experience. Not so! I have come to learn the fallibility of this line of thinking. And if you are on the right side of forty, you too know these are magic years. For those of you who are younger, you are in for the best days of your life.

Wisdom comes with age. And wisdom is there for you to access so that a better understanding of life may begin to unfold. With age, the shrill hysteria of life becomes less audible and life becomes more manageable. The pressures of the twenties and thirties no longer make such harsh and unreasonable demands upon you and you start to inhale and exhale to a more harmonious rhythm of living. Like a colorful blossom slowly opening on a warm summer morning, this is the age for you to shine. The forties—and beyond—reveal a kinder, gentler you. You become kinder to yourself and gentler with others.

I used to fear the forties and beyond, but now I live them and am content and fulfilled. I hope you are doing the same. And if you have yet to reach this wonderful age, try to live like you have—live with wisdom, with enthusiasm, with distinction.

Hurrah for the right side of forty!

Endless Love

Give thanks to the Lord, for he is good. His love endures forever.

PSALM 136:1

I guess what everyone wants more than anything else is to be loved.

ELLA FITZGERALD

Trying to search for the end of God's love is a staggering—and fruitless—quest. His love endures forever. What a stunning thought, that we are loved so completely!

In our human relationships, we ride the roller coaster of emotions that are a common part of intimacy. We fall in and out of love. But it is not so with God. He loves us and His love is endless. We are bedazzled as we encounter true Love and we are consumed with awe that His love for us is so infinite. Like God's mercy, which will never go away, so is His devotion. God is Love and there is nothing that can separate us from Him.

If you want love, start with God. You can trust Him. You do not have to sustain God's love. Nor do you need to coerce Him into loving you. It is the easiest relationship you will ever encounter in your life. And as you revel in His inexhaustible and pleasurable love, you will be renewed and born again. Your outlook will be refreshed. Your walk with Him will strengthen. Your heart will be made brand new.

Love shall liberate you in a divine metamorphosis.

God will love us forever. And the tremendous longing within each of us for love will be fulfilled when we embrace heaven's heartbeat and mesmerize our spirits through meditating on this truth. Daily, let us keep our sacred appointment to become intimately acquainted with the glorious, liberating force of God's endless love.

Dream Weaver

*Where there is no vision, the people perish: but he that keep-
eth the law, happy is he.*

PROVERBS 29:18 (KJV)

Vision is the art of seeing things invisible.

JONATHAN SWIFT

People who refuse to dream close the window of their imagina-
tion, from which dreams travel. Dreams are the forerunner of any
big event. Without dreams, there is no reality.

Do you know what you want? Have you thought it through?
Explored the possibilities? Set goals? Determined that you will
achieve them? Sometimes you must sit down and wrestle with
yourself until you know the answers to these questions. Maybe
you once had a dream and let that dream vanish. Or maybe you
dreamed a dream, accomplished it, and now are ready to dream
again.

When you dream, because you have dared to dream—because
you have chosen to seek for more than what you presently pos-

sess—your very desire, coupled with your expectancy and fortified with a strong work ethic, will set you in a place to receive. Dream again and dream until your dream is fulfilled.

It was Hannah's lack that caused her to dream (1 Sam. 1-20). Her misery, provoked by the taunting of Peninnah, caused her to dream and to pray. Hannah and Peninnah were the wives of Elkanah. Peninnah had children and Hannah had none. Hannah's barrenness, in an era and culture that applauded and celebrated motherhood, fueled her dream. She longed for a child of her own. And so she spun her dream until God answered her prayer and gave her a child—Samuel.

Yes, it's sometimes difficult to make dreams reality because dream weaving is hard work. But it's not impossible. So whatever you are dreaming, keep the vision before you, dream against the odds, find a promise in the Word of God that supports your vision, and like Hannah continue relentlessly in your pursuit until your dream becomes your reality.

Behold, the Dreamer Cometh

Where there is no vision, the people perish.

PROVERBS 29:18 (KJV)

A dream doesn't become reality through magic; it takes sweat, determination, and hard work.

COLIN POWELL

It is a good thing to dream. But sometimes our dreams are for our own enjoyment and would not be understood by others. Therefore, when God places enchanting and magical pictures in your heart, it might be better not to share them with everyone. It is imperative that you flee negative and critical people lest you become like Joseph, who was ridiculed for his vision.

Critical people are dream killers. If they suspect you aspire to higher ground or a better life or some great goal, they will apply the crab maneuver on you. The crab maneuver is when one crab sees another crab starting to ascend and pulls it back down. These types of people will use their speech to bring you down, either through ridicule or by negative affirmation—telling you how impossible your dream is to achieve. Flee from them mentally, physically, and emotionally, fiercely guarding what God has placed in your spirit.

Jochebed, Moses' mother, was a woman of vision. It took courage to hold to her dream to see her son Moses' life spared. Realizing that her baby faced possible death from exposure as he sailed down the Nile, or even annihilation by crocodiles and snakes, she still held fast to her dream and took a risk rather than witness his certain death at the hands of the Egyptians. God rewarded her for her faith and for acting on that faith. She didn't just fantasize about her situation, but skillfully brought into reality what she saw in her spirit. She was rewarded not only by seeing her baby live, but by rising to the position of his nursemaid and receiving wages for raising her own child. How masterful the plan of God!

Whatever you are dreaming about, hold fast to it. Guard it, nourish it, and work hard to see its implementation. Your dream may be the difference between your demise and your absolute success.

You're a Doll!

After she had given him a drink, she said, "I'll draw water for your camels too, until they have finished drinking." So she quickly emptied her jar into the trough, ran back to the well to draw more water, and drew enough for all his camels.

GENESIS 24:19-20

Nothing makes you like other human beings so much as doing things for them.

ZORA NEALE HURSTON

I often respond to those delightful ladies who always seem to live with a spirit of excellence with the words, "You're a doll!"

You're a doll when you keep peace in tumultuous situations—when you're cheery and helpful to others. When you actively seek to do good. Dolls are not necessarily delicate, as are some of their miniature playtime counterparts, but rather hardworking women with no hidden agendas who seek to maintain a light and kind spirit. Dolls are pleasantly supportive, generating positive energy. They are a constant source of encouragement. Dolls stand out because of their commitment to create a bright and cheerful atmosphere. They are always noticeable, like beams of bright sunlight in dark spaces.

Dolls have sunny dispositions, and their optimistic attitudes are the composition of their foundations. Dolls have generous spirits and do for other people without wanting anything in return. They are charming and delightful, innocent and easygoing ladies.

Do you see why being a doll is a distinctive goal? All of us are dolls sometimes. But the challenge is to live the life of a doll *all* the time. It is a worthy goal.

The next time you see a lady who fits this description, just smile and say, "You're a doll!" Then try to be just like her.

Do Not Disturb!

Be completely humble and gentle; be patient, bearing with one another in love. Make every effort to keep the unity of the Spirit through the bond of peace.

EPHESIANS 4:2-3

Holiness is not the luxury of a few. It is everyone's duty: yours and mine.

MOTHER TERESA

You would not slam doors, bang pots and pans, or blast the radio or television if someone were resting or sleeping, would you? I hope not. Most of us are very respectful of each other during quiet times. But how many of us are aware we should respect each other's waking moments to this same degree? And in that light, how many of us have even thought about how important it is to not say or do things to disturb each other's *emotional* peace with an unkind word, ugly insinuation, or vicious rumor that disturbs one's frame of mind and mars the soul.

Remember, each encounter with another individual is an

opportunity for you to show respect and to honor. Practice daily to speak peace wherever you can, remain silent when it is necessary, and regard each soul you encounter as precious and valuable. You and I must strive to master our thoughts and behavior. If the words you speak will not lift up, do not speak them. As you develop into a woman who sheds light and spreads a loving atmosphere, practice gliding like sunlight through the days of others, greeting them with words of encouragement and blessing, remembering above all not to do or say anything to disturb the peace of their souls.

Shhhh!

There You Go,
Acting Like Your Daddy

But I tell you: Love your enemies and pray for those who persecute you.

MATTHEW 5:44

Jesus comes to meet us. To welcome him, let us go to meet him. He comes to us in the hungry, the naked, the lonely, the alcoholic, the drug addict, the prostitute, the street beggar.

MOTHER TERESA

Jesus set up His kingdom in the midst of a generation that resembled every aspect of evil the Church fights so hard against today. Yet He stood in the midst of all that and told us to love our enemies.

I wonder how many of us would last in that kind of environment. Faced with Christ's experiences, would you be able to practice the principles he taught?

Today the Church can barely fulfill Jesus' Great Commission—we can hardly even love one another in the body of Christ, much less the ones who persecute us. How far we seem to be from what He had in mind for us. When we are seen as the hatemongers rallying against those who believe and behave differently from us, we are not acting like our daddy. When we are the ones showing intolerance and indifference to the poor, the imprisoned, and the downtrodden, we are not doing what Christ left us to do.

Let us be found by Christ when He returns going about doing good—loving the unlovely. It is what He did while on this earth and it is what He expects to find us doing when He returns.

CLOUT WITH THE KING

For the Lord God is a sun and shield; the LORD bestows favor and honor; no good thing does he withhold from those whose walk is blameless.

PSALM 84:11

Favor and honor sometimes fall more fitly on those who do not desire them.

TITUS LIVIUS

You may be oblivious to one of the most powerful possessions one could ask for. If you have endured many ordeals with the Lord God at your side and have watched Him bring you faithfully through to the other side, seemingly you would not need anyone to draw your attention to the fact that you have influence with the King. And yet sometimes that is just the case. As a daughter of the Most High, is it possible that you receive the continual endorsement of God and yet let His preferential treatment go unacknowledged?

Sometimes we need miniature wake-up calls to draw our attention to how much we are blessed and how deeply we are loved. Whenever others seek to emulate your life, it is Life nudging you to pay attention to the spiritual pampering and coddling you receive. If you are continually the recipient of jealousy and envy, begin examining your life to discover the reason. Are others more aware of your level of blessing than you?

Often our walk with God is so intimate we don't notice that others do not receive the same approval and indulgences that seem to come to us so naturally. Sometimes we're so bogged down in the battles of life we don't realize that the very fact we are habitually triumphant is a clear indicator that we have clout with God. This is a disproportionate response! And the day may come when, because of our lack of response, our favor is withdrawn.

Woman of God, bow before Him and acknowledge His graciousness, that you would find favor in His sight.

CHRISTMAS MAGIC

Give, and it will be given to you. A good measure, pressed down, shaken together and running over, will be poured into your lap. For with the measure you use, it will be measured to you.

LUKE 6:38

At Christmas play and make good cheer, for Christmas comes but once a year.

THOMAS TUSSER

It doesn't matter what season we're in, I get pleasure thinking of Christmas. I look forward to its arrival and reminisce about it after it has passed. For me, excitement about the holidays seems natural. I'm sure you feel the same. Christmastime finds us caught up in a whirlwind of gift buying and giving, of baking tasty treats to share with friends and family, of taking the time to reflect on our appreciation of each other.

But what about every other day of the year? How can we possess the spirit of Christmas year round? The only avenue I am sure of is through giving. You can know the wonder and excitement of a perpetual Christmas by doing uplifting things for others. Give love. Give gifts. Give yourself away. Remember it is not about the cost of the gifts or the amount of money spent. It is about the act, the deed, the effort. You will be spellbound by the enormous satisfaction and mystique that surrounds you when you open your hand to make someone else happy.

Next Christmas, do yourself a favor and make the atmosphere explode in love. Then the next day, and the next, and the next, spread as much joy, laughter, and kindness as you can.

Children Are the Flowers of Life—Don't Crush Them!

Lo, children are an heritage of the Lord: and the fruit of the womb is his reward.

PSALM 127:3 (KJV)

What feeling is so nice as a child's hand in yours? So small, so soft and warm, like a kitten huddling in the shelter of your clasp.

MARJORIE HOLMES

The gleeful, unrehearsed clamor that bubbles forth from our children is a delight to our ears. Happy little boys and girls lift and release us—distract us from life's contrasting picture.

As a mother and grandmother, it brings me great joy to watch children. As I'm sure it does you. We love their jovial outbursts, their crying jags before naps or mealtime, and their ability to burst into song without notice in the middle of a church service or quiet restaurant—to the delight of everyone within range. Children make us smile. They certainly make us kinder.

Our little ones bless the environment with their innocence. They are heavenly gifts to be cherished, nurtured, and guided. They are the hope of our future. The pleasantness of our tomorrow. They are like the twinkling of a million stars flung across a darkened sky. They are our field of flowers, scenting the fragrance of our lives. Woe be unto this earth if we are ever without them.

My brothers and I recently buried our mother. Our mother put her best into us. She raised us with the tenacity and seriousness of a student attending medical school. It never occurred to her to play around or take lightly her chance to shape and develop our minds and vision. But she was ultimately rewarded for her efforts, for without her deliberate and calculated impartation, she would not have lived her latter days in the comfort and good care that she received. Had she crushed us through neglect or abuse, she would have reaped what she sowed. But because she planted nurturing and guidance in her "little chickens," as we were sometimes referred to, she harvested those same values in her final days—even during her fight with Alzheimer's.

If you have little flower children blooming around you, tend well your garden. You will see many good days, and many desires fulfilled because you cared so well for them during your season of nurturing and cultivating.

I CAN'T WAIT

But those who hope in the Lord will renew their strength.

ISAIAH 40:31

Such is the state of life, that none are happy but by the antic-ipation of change: the change itself is nothing; when we have made it, the next wish is to change again. The world is not yet exhausted; let me see something tomorrow which I never saw before.

SAMUEL JOHNSON

Do you ever find yourself saying, "Oh, I can't wait!" Or "When will it happen?" Well, good! Great expectations hasten the appearance of what you desire. When you expect something, you foresee its coming—you can envision the thing you desire. It is important, though, to remember that while waiting for what we want, we should be not only patient, but eager. Our patience signifies we are certain we will have what we desire; our eagerness establishes a speedy arrival.

What is it that you cannot wait for? Fan the fire of your wish, for with your breathless anticipation, you keep hope alive. Hope, the anchor of our soul, provides us the endurance and bright outlook necessary to strengthen our faith. Through the collaboration of our emotions and intentions we form an alliance to bring about the desired end.

Whatever you are praying to receive, harmoniously couple that prayer with an exuberant anticipation, remembering that when you pray and believe that you will receive, you shall have it.

What is it you can't wait for? Get ready—you shall have it!

Awake, My Love

And to know the love of Christ, which passeth knowledge,
that ye might be filled with all the fulness of God.

EPHESIANS 3:19 (KJV)

Love liberates everything.

MAYA ANGELOU

Would you like to feel energized? Revitalized? Restored? I don't know many people who would not. But focusing on the wrong issues or looking in the wrong direction won't get you where you need to be. Perhaps you need to take stock of things. Does your inner vision need a window washing?

Today I encourage you to continually renew the spirit of your mind. We have heavenly treasures in this earthly realm. Love is in us. Love is all around us. We need only be reminded of our eternal covenant of love with our heavenly Father. As we behold the remarkable goodness of God and as we ponder His exquisite loving kindness unto us, we awake to soul-confirming love. See it everywhere, feel it in your every pore. Our intimate bond with the God who is Love breaks us free from slumber, loosed to arise like cool mist on a still morning lake.

Magnify love. Pass it on so that others may feel what you feel and come to know the love of Christ.

True Riches

*Don't I have the right to do what I want with my own money?
Or are you envious because I am generous?*

MATTHEW 20:15

Money should circulate like rainwater.

THORNTON WILDER

People who teach that money is an evil we should shun are not in touch with reality.

Does it shock you that I say this? It shouldn't. But let me put it into perspective. Money in and of itself is neutral. It is a means to an end. It certainly deserves a place in our lives, but we should understand its order of importance. When we understand like E. M. Bounds that "Money is the lowest form of power," we can acknowledge that although money is useful, it is not the universal god that some regard it to be.

Money can only be appreciated in the light of the true riches of this earthly realm. The love of family, the joy of living, the peace of days, the music of laughter—these are the things that help put money in its rightful place. When we focus on these blessings, it suddenly becomes less important whether we have lots of money or not. If we don't have money, we can work toward earning it while enjoying what we do have. If we do have money, we can use it to help others have a more enjoyable life. So enjoy it. Spend it. Save it. Invest it. Multiply it. Give it away. By circulating it, you are using it for the currency that it is. Let it flow.

What Is That in Your Hand?

———❧———

He took her by the hand and said to her, "Talitha koumi!"
(which means, "Little girl, I say to you, get up!").

MARK 5:41

The fragrance always stays in the hand that gives the rose.

HADA BEJAR

I can pretty much assure you that whatever you need to improve
the quality of your life is in your hand. You and I possess those
things necessary to get up and get on with our lives. It's just that
sometimes we're a little blind to our potential. It's not that we
don't have what we need. Our trouble is in recognizing that what
we seek is already within our possession.

I have seen many people exist on substandard wages because
they will not quench the fire of their pride and ask someone they
don't know well or don't care much about for gainful employment. It takes courage to pursue a goal. The boldness and determination to believe in our worth, our salvation and our Savior, is
equipment enough to possess the land. Accomplishing any goal

also requires making an accurate assessment of your possessions. Taking inventory of your natural abilities and talents is necessary work, but work that will provide a clear picture of your resources.

Have you watched people who need something or who want a specific thing sit idly by as opportunity after opportunity passes? Are you that person? If you are—if you're in an environment where you are observing but not obtaining what you need—then you may not be utilizing what is in your hand. Become aggressive. Let go of fear and reach out and connect to whatever you want and need. If you are special enough to warrant salvation, then you are worthy of receiving and obtaining everything that has been made available to you through redemption. Read your Bible. Find those Scriptures that let you know all the wonderful and good things available to you. It is a sure way to victory.

JUST BECAUSE

Now the Lord is the Spirit, and where the Spirit of the Lord is, there is freedom.

2 CORINTHIANS 3:17

None who have always been free can understand the terrible fascinating power of the hope of freedom to those who are not free.

PEARL S. BUCK

Isn't it nice to do something—anything—just because? Doing something for no other reason than the fact that you can is reason enough.

You and I must take advantage of the many generous freedoms and opportunities available to us. Just because. The liberty to decide and to take action is a prized and precious jewel. We have myriad privileges to enjoy. Take nothing for granted—from the water running freely through your faucet to spending your days coming and going as you please.

Today this country has been threatened by terrorists who likewise seek to steal our freedom and rob us of peace. We have suffered the Attack on America. What many African Americans have long understood, every American now identifies with: freedom is priceless. Taking for granted the good things in life—the ability to come and go and do as we please—is now viewed as obscene.

Not too many years ago in this country, the black experience was wrapped in bondage. A slave's very existence was defined by the wishes of other people. Slaves were not privileged to decide how they would spend their day. Can you imagine yourself waking up every day of your life not having the right to decide if you will go to work, attend school, stay at home to clean, sleep late, play golf, bake, read, or visit a friend or relative? You and I can sing a song, write a letter, shop, stroll through a park, plant a garden. We can venture out. In contrast, a slave's entire existence was filled with affliction and confinement.

Likewise, today there are also people who spend their lives incarcerated in penal institutions where every day is the same as the last. Others have medical conditions that don't allow them the opportunity of a lifestyle that includes freedoms so many others enjoy. It might not be quite the same thing as a life of slavery, but to them it might sometimes feel so.

I challenge you: because you do have the ability and the right to choose, do something in honor of those who can't. Do for those who are unable to do. Do it simply because you can.

Just because.

STRUGGLES

NOT BEFORE IT'S TIME

Therefore judge nothing before the appointed time.

1 CORINTHIANS 4:5

I was the only Negro woman in my dental school class, and I was mighty lonely, but I didn't let that stop me. I wanted to be the best dentist that ever lived. People said, "But she's a woman; she's colored." And I said, "Ha! Just you wait and see."

BESSIE DELANY

The farmer knows what many parents need to hear. It takes time to see results. Tilling the ground, sowing the seed, watering the tender shoots, and nurturing the plant is work that takes place over a period of time.

So it is with parenting. It will be a long time before you see the fruit of your labor. In spite of the high-tech, cyberspace generation in which we reside, you and I cannot fast-forward the seasons, nor the times. Life is not like that. It is erroneous to think that all things come instantaneously. We've become so conditioned to microwave-fast solutions, we want to microwave the process of development. It won't happen.

My own mother didn't get to see real results from her own parenting until we were in our thirties and forties. I'm sure there were times along the way she thought she'd failed completely. I'm sure there were times she thought it would never end. But she finally had the opportunity to see the adults she had created. Hopefully it was worth the wait.

Rest assured that when you do the important and necessary work of parenting and do it well, you will have the satisfaction of knowing that in the fullness of time, you will see the rewarding results. Be patient!

Tell Somebody!

*They ravished the women in Zion, and the maids in the cities
of Judah. Princes are hanged up by their hand: the faces of
elders were not honoured. They took the young men to grind,
and the children fell under the wood. The elders have ceased
from the gate, the young men from their musick. The joy of
our heart is ceased; our dance is turned into mourning.*

LAMENTATIONS 5:11-15 (KJV)

Silence gives consent.

OLIVER GOLDSMITH

As handmaidens of the kingdom, as queens of the King, we
sometimes erroneously assume that because we are made to be
partakers of our glorious liberty in Christ Jesus, all is well and has
always been well with each one of us. It is not so.

Sadly, for some—for many, actually—there have been times of
great and grinding darkness. For centuries there have been mil-
lions of secret survivors of molestation, incest, and rape. It is so

commonplace that I find it mandatory to write to you, the possible victim of such a monstrous and atrocious activity.

First, I apologize to you. May I be perhaps the first person to say to you, "I am very sorry that something so outrageously vicious happened to you."

Second, may I encourage you to please find someone trustworthy, someone responsible, someone caring and loving and tell them. Tell somebody so that you may release yourself from the bondages of the unspoken pact that continues to bind you with your assailant. You no longer need to keep quiet their violation of you. God has made provisions for every hurt, every injustice, and every disease. He provides a healing balm in the people of God, physicians, and therapists who stand by waiting to pour oil and wine onto your wounds that you may be healed of your memories, your bruised emotions, and your damaged soul.

This is an opportunity to cleave to the Lord until you are made whole again. The events you have suffered give you the chance to become intimate with Christ and to cast this unbearable burden onto Him. By His own meticulous methods, He will deliver you into wholeness, one step at a time, moment by moment.

As God washes your memories, your heart, and your soul with His love, frequently bathe your thoughts in the knowledge that you are greatly loved and a genuine superhero who can never be conquered by any darkness. You are a valued vessel, priceless in the sight of God.

March On, My Soul. Be Strong!

Finally, be strong in the Lord and in his mighty power.

EPHESIANS 6:10

The fire that seems so cruel is the light that shows your strength.

ELLA WHEELER WILCOX

It was after the sixth of her eight brain surgeries that my mother, a seventy-three-year-old, now one-hundred-pound woman whose will remained strong as her body waned in feebleness, sat visibly trembling. My youngest brother, Tom, whose resolve at that moment was giving way, looked at her through tears of frustration and said, "I don't see how you are handling this!" My mother lifted her bald head and reared her shoulders back and said in a hearty voice, "You do what you have to do, and don't you forget it."

Our mother was right. People who are emotionally strong are sometimes perceived as supernatural. In reality, they simply know a secret their onlookers have yet to discover: their courage lies not within their own strength but in their complete abandonment to the Lord. Strong people have the ability to recognize and embrace the grace they have been given. They keenly recognize their frailties and usually have an impressive résumé of personal accounts of mighty deliverances by the hand of God. Their ability to stand steady and strong, like mighty oak trees that cannot be uprooted or moved, is a natural response. Through much practice, they have become adept at clinging to their Strength. They have unwrapped their gift of grace and carry it with them into each fiery furnace and onto each battlefield.

You may be facing a difficult situation today, and perhaps you feel as weak as water. Take heart! You, too, can know God as your strength and your salvation. Do not draw back; His strength is made perfect in weakness (2 Cor. 12:9). Lift your head, my friend, and do . . . what you have to do!

SOLID ROCK

*But his bow remained steady, his strong arms stayed limber,
because of the hand of the Mighty One of Jacob, because of
the Shepherd, the Rock of Israel, because of your father's
God, who helps you, because of the Almighty, who blesses
you with blessings of the heavens above, blessings of the deep
that lies below, blessings of the breast and womb. Your
father's blessings are greater than the blessings of the ancient
mountains, than the bounty of the age-old hills.*

GENESIS 49:24-26

*On matters of style, swim with the current; on matters of
principle, stand like a rock.*

THOMAS JEFFERSON

When my now adult daughter, Kelly, was but a tiny girl, I sat
her down and told her this: "If there is but one thing I would
want you to remember all the days of your life and never forget,
it would be this: 'On Christ the solid rock I stand; all other
ground is sinking sand.'"

It is crucial to understand that in order to survive the winds of this life, you need only hold fast to what will never change—the abiding presence of the Lord. It is imperative to have no misconceptions about truth, success, or what supposedly really works in this world (according to the "experts").

My bottom line is to continue on with Christ. The reality of Him has been proven in my life. I have passed on to my daughter what my mother passed on to my brothers and me—that Jesus is the Way, the Truth, and the Light. It is my belief in Him that has brought me over rough terrain, through impassable places, and from beneath impenetrable dark clouds.

Your trust in the solidity of Jesus, the Rock, is your life preserver, your light for any dark pathway. In Him you shall triumph, no matter what storm you face.

JUST SHOW UP

On a Sabbath Jesus was teaching in one of the synagogues, and a woman was there who had been crippled by a spirit for eighteen years. She was bent over and could not straighten up at all. When Jesus saw her, he called her forward and said to her, "Woman, you are set free from your infirmity." Then he put his hands on her, and immediately she straightened up and praised God.

LUKE 13:10-13

Courage is very important. Like a muscle, it is strengthened by use.

RUTH GORDON

Being in the right place at the right time and having something good happen to you is more about persistence than about chance.

The woman who was healed on the Sabbath received her healing because she chose to continue living despite her severe deformity. She was not hiding in obscurity. She was getting around. She stood bravely before the Lord in a bowed position that probably resembled a permanent curtsy. She could not have enjoyed being seen in such a condition, yet she chose to be among the other believers in the synagogue.

Completely visible in the crowd, she was put on further display when Jesus called her out. How she must have felt to suddenly see all eyes turned on her! But the reward she received was far greater than any momentary embarrassment could ever have been. For before she could even call out to God, He answered her secret prayer. This woman was healed simply because she showed up.

Too often we lull ourselves into a place of nonparticipation in life and therefore forfeit our opportunities for growth and advancement. To stay in the game of life means we must have the courage to become involved. Our sheer determination to stay active and to not shrink into the shadows is what nets us favorable results to further enliven and mellow our existence.

You, or someone you know, may struggle with an emotional or physical disability that restrains you and negates your interest in venturing out. May I encourage you today to push past your struggle as much as you can? Having the courage to go out, even on a very limited basis, will loose the chains of confinement and give you the miracle of renewal that refreshes and sweetens your life.

As Promised

"For I know the plans I have for you," declares the Lord, "plans to prosper you and not to harm you, plans to give you hope and a future."

JEREMIAH 29:11

Two things everybody's got to do for themselves: They've got to trust God, and they've got to find out about living for themselves.

ZORA NEALE HURSTON

Resting on and believing in a promise brings relief to an anguished soul. A promise we know will be fulfilled is a spiritual stressbuster. We find renewal in blessed assurances. Good words like *prosper*, *hope*, and *future* prompt us to continue on. Our hope is restored in spite of what may be going on in our lives. Our insight has been renewed as we stand on the promises of God.

To caress the face of a promise in the midst of adversity is a monumental but realistic task. As we touch the heart of hope through a promise, we are born again in the center of our being.

We are made brand new from healing words. What a delight to believe all things are possible. That good things are possible. We are transported to childhood expectation and wonder.

Seek daily to import into your spirit the promises of God. Dwell in the Word, which details those promises. Whisper them in your prayers as a reminder of them. Speak them aloud to others. When, like the feather of a strong eagle that has dislodged itself from the wing and floats in slow motion—uncaring and unconcerned—we let go and let God take over, resting in Him and trusting in His care, we too are allowed to float free so that we may go on to do the things that give life, to ourselves and to others.

He has promised.

Physician, Heal Thyself!

Is not this the kind of fasting I have chosen: to loose the chains of injustice and untie the cords of the yoke, to set the oppressed free and break every yoke? Is it not to share your food with the hungry and to provide the poor wanderer with shelter—when you see the naked, to clothe him, and not to turn away from your own flesh and blood? Then your light will break forth like the dawn, and your healing will quickly appear.

ISAIAH 58:6-8

The lamp burns bright when wick and oil are clean.

H. P. BLAVATSKY

People blame their conditions on what they can see. And therefore they sometimes erroneously attribute maladies, disappointments, and depressions to unrelated issues. And likewise good health. But there is a sacred tie between heaven and earth, the spiritual and the natural, the celestial and the terrestrial, and it isn't always obvious.

Would you naturally make the connection between a healing and helping others? It's true. In each of us there is predisposed DNA that determines, among many other things, the state of our health. It seems too simple to think that a change in our attitude and behavior brings about a change in our bodies, but that is exactly what the Scriptures declare. To get our minds off of ourselves and to become involved in the well-being and welfare of others can bring about our own speedy deliverance. If we can change our DNA, our medical conditions, through lending someone else a hand, then we should do it.

You have been invited to love your way into health. Become your sister's keeper and love her as yourself—it will renew you and restore you. Today, make the connection between helping and your health. You don't have a minute to waste. Someone needs you.

PARENTING

Children, obey your parents in the Lord, for this is right.

EPHESIANS 6:1

The most important thing that parents can teach their children is how to get along without them.

FRANK A. CLARK

One of the hardest, most exhausting, and yet most exhilarating jobs you will ever perform is to parent. I do not think there is a higher calling than this. Those who take the time and effort to instruct, nurture, and love their children will be rewarded throughout the ages.

The benefits of good parenting far outweigh any professional endeavors you will pursue. The lasting effect of a well-done project at work will impact your life transiently—praise from your coworkers, perhaps a raise. But the lasting effect of a parenting job well done will follow you to your grave.

My brothers and I recently buried our mother, our only surviving parent. The teaching she imparted and the care she gave to us made her last days on earth quite victorious. Had she not bothered to rear us well, it would have met her in her illness and during her last few months on this earth. But because she had made it her business to instill good, strong qualities into each of her children, she was laid safely to rest by the works of her own hands and the fruits of her own labor.

As you parent, it is so important you do your work well. You are shaping your child's life and very possibly your future. It is imperative that you impart every bit of wisdom, guidance, and teaching you can to your offspring. This doesn't always mean direct, verbal interaction—you would be amazed at what your children will pick up from your actions and your attitude. Creating an atmosphere of love, discipline, respect, and order provides a sure foundation.

Remember, like a school course that ultimately concludes with an exam, you will one day be graded on your current efforts. Making the sacrifice, doing the hard things through parenting while it is your season to do so, will allow you to have the peace of a bright future for your children and perhaps comfort and security for yourself in your latter days.

The work you have done in secret, behind closed doors, in the privacy of your home with your children, will be manifested. Now's your chance to make sure it will manifest in a positive and not a negative way!

Never Give Up

With God all things are possible.

MATTHEW 19:26

The future belongs to those who see possibilities before they become obvious.

UNKNOWN

What are the chances of a man who has been maliciously locked in prison for twenty-seven years coming out without hate and bitterness and rising to be elected president of the country that ensnared and incarcerated him? Think it couldn't happen? Remember Nelson Mandela?

What are the chances of a country girl, a coal miner's daughter, becoming a country-western singer superstar. A long shot? You've heard of Loretta Lynn, haven't you?

What are the chances of a young Jewish girl raised in the midwestern United States heading the state of Israel. Do you think it not possible? The name Golda Meir should be familiar to you.

What are the chances of a little girl who was raised by her

grandmother in abject poverty, was sexually molested by family and a friend of the family, and ended up a pregnant teen rising to become one of America's most famous and wealthy women and the queen of talk shows. Think it isn't possible? You've heard of Oprah Winfrey, haven't you?

What are the chances of a small-town preacher teaching a small Sunday school class of forty women and having that class grow to an annual conference drawing nearly eighty thousand women from around the world. Think it's unlikely? Do you know Bishop T. D. Jakes?

Very few of us today face such extenuating challenges or small beginnings. But that doesn't mean what you *are* going through isn't important and disheartening. Whatever your situation, take these examples as your inspiration. No matter what you are facing, despite the dismal forecast, you cannot count yourself down and out.

Never give up! The most impossible and hopeless situation can be turned around.

MUCH ADO ABOUT NOTHING

Hear me, O God, as I voice my complaint; protect my life from the threat of the enemy.

PSALM 64:1

Our doubts are traitors, and make us lose the good that we oft may win, by fearing to attempt.

WILLIAM SHAKESPEARE

One tactic of deception the enemy has for our lives is the use of threats. Like the children of Israel escaping amidst the thunder of Pharaoh's chariots, we are often found running for our lives from things sent to worry us and make us fearful. But I would challenge you, like the title of Tammy Faye Bakker's book, to "Run to the Roar." As the shepherd boy David told Goliath as he ran toward that giant, "I come at you in the name of the Lord" (1 Sam. 17:45). You and I must be confident in our walk with God that He is able to hide us when necessary, guide us at all times, and expose our strength in perhaps unexpected ways to defeat any enemy in our lives.

Do not lose your focus—I caution you not to look at anything that seeks to immobilize you through fear. The Lord has told us His thoughts and plans for us are for good and not for evil. We need to hold on to that and allow it to comfort us!

In order to bring more comfort and peace into your life, think on the goodness of Jesus and all that He has done for you. Today, if you hear hoofbeats at your heels, constantly bring to your remembrance that you are safe with God. His name alone is "a strong tower; the righteous run to it and are safe" (Prov. 18:10).

Like Jesus, we must be about our Father's business, spending our lives glorifying God, helping others, and not giving heed to much ado about nothing.

IT DOESN'T MATTER

I know what it is to be in need, and I know what it is to have plenty. I have learned the secret of being content in any and every situation, whether well fed or hungry, whether living in plenty or in want. I can do everything through him who gives me strength.

PHILIPPIANS 4:12-13

You don't get to choose how you're going to die, or when. You can only decide how you're going to live now.

JOAN BAEZ

One of the quickest ways to determine what is important in this life is to experience trouble on a catastrophic level. If you have ever had a face-to-face encounter with horrendous hurt or danger, it is hard to take seriously any petty annoyances. You might occasionally entertain nuisances, but you do not see the minor struggles and challenges of day-to-day living as anything but mild irritations.

As a member of a very large ministry, I encounter every type of situation, from personality clashes to deadline pressures to nearly every imaginable struggle that faces mankind, from illness to midlife crisis! I've seen it all. Some of these delimmas are important, but many of them are simply squabbles and ego issues or minor problems that are easily solved and perhaps don't warrant the attention they are afforded.

But then I see something like what happened during the terrorist attacks of September 11, 2001. And when I do, I am instantly put into my place. Compared to what is happening in the lives of those affected in that catastrophic event, almost nothing else has importance—at least not the things I just spoke about!

The next time you are tempted to whine about and criticize whatever is going on in your home, work, or school, remember that it probably doesn't matter as much as you think it does. Remember that there are far more severe problems in the world that deserve your fervent attention. The next time you find your temper flaring or watch someone else grow angry about something relatively insignificant, instead of reacting negatively, simply take a moment to silently thank God for His mercies. I promise you'll feel better by providing your own reality check.

All the Lonely Women

What I see brings grief to my soul because of all the women of my city.

LAMENTATIONS 3:51

Love all the people you can. The sufferings from love are not to be compared to the sorrows of loneliness.

SUSAN HALE

"All the lonely people—where do they all come from?" In the sixties the Beatles sang a song asking that question. Today we live in the dawn of a new millennium, and that age-old question remains unanswered. All the lonely women!

Today women don't need men so much to take care of them—that philosophy has hopefully disappeared with this new generation—but more to celebrate life with. To share their lives with. But having and holding someone has become a bit of a challenge in this day and age. Somehow, in our emphasis on education and moving on up, we lost track of some of the things that really matter. Like who we would like to share the new Lexus (or Kia!) with and who will live with us in the big house on the hill and who will go flying off to exotic islands and sugar-white beaches with us. We've spent years climbing the ladder. Now that we've arrived, isn't it time we had someone with whom to celebrate? Are we finding that success isn't so fun when we have no one to share it with?

These questions are not easily answered. Perhaps you're not even ready to think about answering them. But if you are ready and are having trouble finding that special someone, I urge you to keep your playing field open. Don't give up. Broaden your range; explore new types of suitors that perhaps you hadn't considered before. And most of all, stay open, alive, and vibrantly happy.

Your prince is out there!

You Are Not Your Kneecaps

The blind receive sight, the lame walk, those who have leprosy are cured, the deaf hear, the dead are raised, and the good news is preached to the poor.

MATTHEW 11:5

Not everything that can be counted counts, and not everything that counts can be counted.

ALBERT EINSTEIN

What do I mean when I say "You are not your kneecaps"? Well, I mean that although the outside packaging may become altered, what's inside is what truly matters. For example, the war veteran that returns home disfigured and misshapen is still inwardly the same person—because he is more than kneecaps, arms, legs, a face, or a shoulder. Just like you and I, the physically challenged, the burn victim, the disfigured are spiritual beings housed in earthly bodies, no matter what those bodies may look like.

If you have ever suffered and survived some physical, mental, or emotional devastation, you probably already know that who you are on the inside remained intact during your healing process, regardless of what your outside looked like. For those of you who haven't gone through a catastrophe, let me assure you that while we are all human beings, the real us behind the outer shell of our bodies never changes. The packaging may become altered, but we are not our kneecaps.

Human beings are spirit first. We are merely wrapped in a body so that we may survive the unique atmosphere of this planet. But it is our emotions and feelings that express our souls. This is the kind of knowledge that helps us reach out to and understand others who for some reason or another must live out their life in a marred or immobile earth suit. If some calamity occurred in your own life, you would want others to know only the outer wrapping had been damaged, but inside was still a beautiful and perfectly stunning human being.

Imperfections make us appear to be valueless. This society and culture is erroneously preoccupied with outward beauty, spending inordinate amounts of time, money, and worry on what will eventually perish. The flesh. The skin. The face, hair, teeth, kneecaps. The spotlight should instead shine on what is really important, and that is who we are on the inside. Our real treasure is hidden within us. Jesus came for those who need a physician because He knew all men have value, and not just the ones who appear to look good, normal, or perfect. His death was not for the physically attractive or only those with perfectly formed bodies. He died to set men's souls free.

Who we truly are is behind the veil of flesh. Do not be deceived when you see someone physically marred. Quickly, remember the merits of his or her soul.

He Is There!

*Yea, though I walk through the valley of the shadow of death,
I will fear no evil: for thou art with me; thy rod and thy staff
they comfort me.*

PSALM 23:4 (KJV)

Faith can put a candle in the darkest night.

MARGARET SANGSTER

Let us not be lulled into thinking that we face our every day alone. That is so untrue. We should take consolation in knowing that God is everywhere. There is nowhere you can be that He is not. He is by your side.

You must take this truth, like a soft blanket to wrap you warmly on a dark and cold night, and drape it around your broken heart, your sufferings, and all life's inadequacies, and confidently snuggle into the soothing presence of God. Just knowing He is with you can safely and calmly bring you through each day. His omnipresence is your strength. Embrace it.

You and I must frequently remind ourselves that God, who controls the universe, is in charge of our affairs, too. Relying on Him to do what He does releases us to do what He has called us to do. Go on. Remember. He is there.

HABITUALLY TRIUMPHANT

But thanks be to God, who always leads us in triumphal pro-
cession in Christ and through us spreads everywhere the fra-
grance of the knowledge of him.

2 CORINTHIANS 2:14

Our greatest glory is not in never failing, but in rising every
time we fall.

CONFUCIUS

We all need the struggles of our lives to be memorialized so that
we can be constantly reminded of the goodness and faithfulness
of God. Somewhere in the pages of time, there should be visible
and invisible markers to indicate those special testimonies of
what God has brought us through. Although our hearts are the
invisible treasure chest that hold near and dear the blessings of
the Lord, tangible treasure chests are significant, too.

Somewhere on a steep mountainside in the hills of West
Virginia lies a huge rock with footsteps hollowed out with a
wooden ax by the strong hand of my father, Ernest Jakes Sr. The

wide rock lies in the middle of a barely visible wooded path, sometimes lined with streams of buttery sunlight. After Daddy hollowed out the footsteps, the indentations became a place where my younger brother, Tommy, could place his feet to steady himself as he climbed over the large mass. From that time on, in his walks to and from school, what had initially been an obstacle to him became a place of triumph each day as he safely maneuvered over the rock.

The people of Israel, too, placed stones in the bottom of the Jordan to indicate a place of victory. They were "to serve as a sign among you. In the future, when your children ask you, 'What do these stones mean?' tell them that the flow of the Jordan was cut off before the ark of the covenant of the Lord. When it crossed the Jordan, the waters of the Jordan were cut off. These stones are to be a memorial to the people of Israel forever" (Josh. 4:6-7).

What place in your life has God carved out for you to safely continue your journey? Today, as you revisit the memorial stones in your life that symbolize the faithfulness of God, be mindful that victory is sure.

Go On!

Better is the end of a thing than the beginning thereof: and the patient in spirit is better than the proud in spirit.

ECCLESIASTES 7:8 (KJV)

When one door of happiness closes, another opens, but often we look so long at the closed door that we do not see the one which has been opened to us.

HELEN KELLER

What happens to us when we find that life has thrown us a fast-ball, a curve? What are we to do when we find ourselves steeped in some emotional pit or caught up in a web of circumstances that have us hemmed in like the knot of a tightly tied shoelace?

There is an expression that some of the older Christians used a long time ago during church testimony services: "I think I'll go on and see what the end is going to be." That is exactly what we have to do. We must continue to move in the direction of what we want to see in our lives. Stopping to get caught up where disaster fell or where disappointment reared its unwelcome head is not a good prescription for successful living.

Today, my sister, get up from wherever you are, loose your gaze from the sights that have emotionally paralyzed you, from the direction of discouragement. You ask me how to do this? Let me remind you that you and I have the choice of how we will respond to any situation. The decision to look for and embrace the positive is within our control. Make a promise to yourself that you will not participate in any conspiracy that is launched for your demise.

If you refuse to give up, you will get to where you want to go in this life. I promise.

Go on! Go on! Go on!

GOLD DUST

It was good for me to be afflicted.

PSALM 119:71

Gold has a price, but people are priceless.

CHINESE PROVERB

They are easily spotted. Like shiny, sparkling stars on dark nights, they stand out in stark contrast to the vast majority of society. You may be one of this small, select, and secret society of distinguished individuals. If so, your attitude is upbeat. Your outlook is positive. Small things make you glow. It doesn't take much to make your day; you are constantly thankful.

In my mind, people like the above are pure, glittering gold. Gold that has been melted into glimmering shimmers of liquid light. Having been tried in the smelting pot of affliction, their character is marked with distinction. Strangely enough, they agree with the psalmist David—it *was* good for them that they were afflicted. Turbulent times have made them triumphant. They are better from the unsolicited pain that has personalized them as uniquely as a thumbprint. Alexander David-Neel said it well many years ago when he noted: "Suffering raises up those souls that are truly great." From fool's gold to real gold . . .

We too are blessed by their golden attitudes. From tragic places these same ones have become caretakers for our souls. We all need someone who can really empathize with our plights, someone who can console us when life hurls its tragedies. They have been there. They understand and sympathize. They can help us find our own rich and gold-filled path.

If you are facing some unbearable circumstance, look around you. Gold dust is sprinkled everywhere.

Get in the Game

A sluggard does not plow in season; so at harvest time he looks but finds nothing.

PROVERBS 20:4

You can't get full watching someone else eat.

UCHENDI "CHIN" NWANI

Some things happen. Some things are destined to happen. And then there are those things that you must make happen.

Sitting in the bleachers of life applauding the winners is a nice and polite thing to do. However, it is also nonproductive. You must start somewhere to get onto the playing field of life. Whenever a seemingly elusive venture beckons you, quickly jump off the sidelines and into the game and participate! Far better to take a risk on something you want to see happen than to sit idly by wishing for a better existence and ultimately resenting those folks who acquire things you too desire.

You'll never be satisfied simply watching someone else eat from across your empty plate. You and I want to join people for a homemade dinner, not peer through the sparkling glass of a cafe window watching satisfied consumers making merry.

I will never regret taking my first airline flight at seventeen years old, a few weeks after graduation. I went from the hills of West Virginia to the widely paved streets of Washington, D.C. And there I made a start on a life for myself which I have never regretted and which has served me greatly. I was not content to sit back idly at that tender age and let life pass me by. As a result, the entire course of my life became a wondrous adventure.

You may desire to make a change in your life. You won't be able to do it by thinking about it. Why not get up now and make a move in the direction you want your life to go. Take up your helmet or your bat or your ball and hop into the game. You won't be disappointed!

Exception to the Rule

And there were many in Israel with leprosy in the time of Elisha the prophet, yet not one of them was cleansed—only Naaman the Syrian."

LUKE 4:27

The doctors told me I would never walk, but my mother told me I would—so I believed my mother.

WILMA RUDOLPH

I wonder what you—or someone you love—may be facing today that seems absolutely impossible. Perhaps your situation is hopeless and it's illogical for you to even consider that God might do the unimaginable in your life. If this is the case, take heed: not only does God specialize in doing what seems impossible, not only is He a genius at taking futile situations and turning them completely around, He is notorious for doing so.

Have you ever heard of Naaman? Naaman was a leper. In Old Testament days, once infected, absolutely no one escaped horrible death from the cruel hand of leprosy. No one but Naaman, that is. Through a series of events, Naaman went down in history as the only person in his era to be healed of the vicious disease. That made Naaman an exception to the rule.

Today there are many survivors of deadly killer diseases. Thrivers. So many people in every arena of life have gone up against the odds and won, it is now becoming nearly impossible to think that anything is impossible. So I tell you, it can be done. Whatever your situation, it can be done.

Whatever it is you need today, do yourself a favor and defy the odds. If you have persisted in believing your situation is insurmountable, so much the better—what have you got to lose? Give God a chance to do what He does best. Let Him who is our salvation save you from whatever, wherever, and whomever seeks your demise.

DOUBLE FOR YOUR TROUBLE

The Lord is good, a refuge in times of trouble. He cares for those who trust in him.

NAHUM 1:7

Sweet are the uses of adversity.

WILLIAM SHAKESPEARE

We are often so accepting of life's troubles that when our conflict is finally over we find ourselves so glad to get away that we walk away leaving the spoils on the battlefield.

If you have fought any battles (and I'm sure you have), there are rewards on the table for you. No one goes to war without collecting the spoils. If you don't reap the benefits of your troubles and double the reward for whatever you lost or sacrificed or endured, you're missing out on payday. You are due treasures that come only from adversity.

Your wealth as a believer is unlocked through knowing what is rightfully yours. You are in this earthly realm not only to survive but to thrive. If you are going to thrive, you must have abundance. The thermometer you can use to measure your harvest is the furnace of affliction. The greater the affliction, the greater the reward. Do you seek out trouble? Of course not. But when trouble happens, you have to remember that on the other side of it are good things for you.

When you are faced with adversity, make sure to take refuge in God through prayer. And after you have triumphed, remember to collect double—double health, double prosperity, double love. It's your due!

Don't Sign for That!

Butter and honey shall he eat, that he may know to refuse the evil, and choose the good.

ISAIAH 7:15 (KJV)

Often the test of courage is not to die but to live.

VITTORIO ALFIERI

Accepting packages that don't belong to you is illegal and unethical. We know this in the physical world—are taught it as a child. But what about the emotional or spiritual worlds? In these realms there are often unseen choices delivered to us. When we sign for them without thinking things through, we are prone to make unwise choices purely out of habit and erroneous assumptions. One of the problems in daily living is that we sometimes see everything that comes our way as acceptable. Not necessarily so.

For example, the woman with the issue of blood (Matt. 9:20) was a woman who did not accept what came her way. This woman was by law, because of the nature of her illness, restricted from public places. Yet she refused to accept her medical condition and pressed her way through a crowd to touch the hem of Jesus' garment. Her act of faith caused her deliverance. Had she stayed at home, as required by the laws of her day, and resigned herself to her circumstances, we would never have heard of this great and courageous lady. Her inability to accept what was not hers drove her out of her home and into the streets, to crawl across the ground until she had made contact with the miracle maker, Jesus.

When we have things and circumstances in our lives that do not belong there, we too must defy the odds and do whatever it takes to reach the place that will liberate us from our dilemma.

You may find this radical, but all circumstances are not sent for you to accept. How often have you assumed that because something has happened to you, you should settle for it? True, things that are God's will for you cannot be prayed away. But we have a delivery contract. Read the fine print, and if what has come your way does not line up with God's covenant . . . don't sign for it!

Don't Put Him Out

In all thy ways acknowledge him, and he shall direct thy paths.

PROVERBS 3:6 (KJV)

Toward what should we aim, if not toward God?

ANDRÉ GIDE

Whenever our lives become oversaturated with calamity, the correct response sometimes feels as though it should be to withdraw from people and from God. Guilt and shame that our lives are dishonorably displayed is sometimes too much for us to handle. Going into battle alone, however, is the very last thing you want to do.

Isolation during a storm is a perfect breeding ground for anxiety and fosters a lot of unhealthy thinking. Uneasiness escalates and misconceptions abound when you are not spiritually guided and correctly directed. The confusion that results from a self-appointed quarantine is harmful.

Never put God out of your life. You and I both know you cannot hide from Him anyway. In the midst of your worst struggle, do not become bitter. Many times we are so overcome with fear, guilt, and grief we flee the presence of people and God only to unknowingly multiply our sorrows and leave ourselves without the protection and care we need.

At the height of your worst nightmare or in the face of your most lewd sin, involve God in your affairs. The worse your trouble, the more you should cleave to God. He promises never to leave us or forsake us. He will hide you in His love and cover you with His grace and mercy and cleanse you of all unrighteousness.

Do not be deceived. Never put God out!

The Perfect Hand

How long must I wrestle with my thoughts and every day have sorrow in my heart? How long will my enemy triumph over me?

PSALM 13:2

Someone else could have your hand and win.

T. D. JAKES

It is a frightening and sobering thought to realize the very things we complain about—the hand life has dealt us that we constantly bemoan—another woman could begin to play . . . and win.

Shame on us for lamenting a perfectly winnable hand. Shame on us for wallowing in the ridiculous self-pity that clouds our perception of the strengths we actually possess and keeps us from remembering how blessed we really are.

There are people watching your life right now wishing with all their might they could be you. They would love to have your gifts, sit where you sit, go to the places you go, and have the friends you have. They are waiting for an opportunity to glean the least little bit they can from your existence. Don't be so spoiled you cannot see you have got it going on, girl! Don't be lulled into a slumber that causes you to forget what a priceless jewel you are and the queenly existence God has given you to live.

I challenge you to notice those less fortunate. I watched a man earlier today guiding his electric wheelchair over the sidewalk and across a busy intersection, unassisted. I wondered how he had the courage to perform the task. And I was immediately mindful of my own blessings.

Observe the people around you—those who struggle with financial or physical challenges. Notice those without sufficient food, clean water, decent clothes, or an adequate facility in which to lie down to sleep at night. Notice the woman at the grocery store who stops to count her money before reaching the checkout counter. Notice the man on the street corner holding a sign asking for help. Look at them and remember how blessed you are. Remember how they would most likely do anything to be in your place.

One of the quickest ways to realize your own abundance is by determining that you will achieve whatever dreams you have. You have been favored to do so. It's time to play out your winning hand.

DANCE THE NIGHT AWAY

Lord, be thou my helper. Thou hast turned for me my mourning into dancing: thou hast put off my sackcloth, and girded me with gladness.

PSALM 30:10-11 (KJV)

The dance is a poem of which each movement is a word.

MATA HARI

A few years ago a particular song made its way onto the Christian music charts: "Don't Wait until the Battle Is Over—Shout Now." You can tell the message of the song from its title; hope resonates from each ringing musical note and uplifting word of encouragement. It is a good prescription. While we wait for the manifestation of answered prayer or battle the darkness of a personal trial, let's shout, sing, and dance. Chasing the gloom away with praise and rejoicing before a victory is even won is not an uncommon practice. The advice is as old as the walls of Jericho the children of Israel saw tumbling down during their glorious shout.

Having the strength to celebrate before the outcome is a mighty act of faith. With this mind-set, believing is seeing. Remember, you have a choice as to how you respond to the seasons of darkness and trial in your life. You don't have to be unhappy, especially if you believe you are only one act of praise, one shout, one dance away from victory.

So, dear reader, as you face your night, remember the psalmist David and dance, dance, dance . . .

Broken Promises, Shattered Dreams

And the rest, some on boards, and some on broken pieces of the ship. And so it came to pass, that they escaped all safe to land.

ACTS 27:44

Dreams are the touchstones of our characters.

HENRY DAVID THOREAU

Experience is a powerful teacher. If many of your experiences are distressful, negative, or painful, it can become a breeding ground for depression. If your unfilled dreams have turned into nightmares that haunt you and overwhelm you with visions of broken promises and unhappy endings, the tendency to become hopeless and to give up becomes dominant. It seems appropriate to despair. Right?

Wrong!

Who told you divorce was the end of romance for you? Who

declared your age is the barometer for the release or denial of your desired blessings? What made you think your surgery marked the end of the quality of your living? Where is it written in cement that you cannot and will not be allowed to finish your degree?

Because some things have not happened in your life does not mean they never will occur. When God allows a *Selah*—a pause or place of reflection in your life—do not accept it as the cessation of everything. You are only at a temporary impasse. Perhaps the direction in which you were going has changed, but your life has not terminated. Your delay should not be perceived as a denial of your dreams, only an interruption. Take advantage of it!

Whether or not your future is clearly visible to you at this time, it is a good time to consider how Martha, the sister of Lazarus, reacted to Jesus after her brother lay dead for four days: "But I know that even now God will give you whatever you ask" (John 11:22). She knew that even then Jesus could raise Lazarus. Don't let what appears to be an end-of-the-road experience lead you to forfeit hope for all that you desire. Even now your dreams can come true. Even now your broken promises can be healed.

Selah.

DON'T PUSH THE PANIC BUTTON

Do not be anxious about anything, but in everything, by prayer and petition, with thanksgiving, present your requests to God.

PHILIPPIANS 4:6

I never really look for things. I accept whatever God throws my way. Whichever way God turns my feet, I go.

PEARL BAILEY

Generally, things always look better in the morning.

That's a good thought to remember, because occasionally we have those days where everything seems to go haywire. The toilet overflows, the dog runs out the gate as you're leaving for work, you lose your wallet or your expensive watch, or the car won't start. Instead of money in the mail, your bank statement shows bounced checks. Past-due bills have gone to collection and it's hours before bedtime and you're wondering what will happen next. It's enough to send you scurrying to hide under the covers.

You have to keep things in perspective. It's life. It's mismanagement. It's nuisances. And it's going to get better and it's going to go away. What's important is to keep your head straight in the midst of distractions that vie like circus acts for your attention and attempt to throw you off balance. Stop. Steady yourself and slowly bring to mind that you are too blessed to be stressed. Remember: God tells us not to be anxious about anything. So chill.

Reacting hysterically to life's challenges will not help you acquire the sense of resolve you need right now. Second by second, life changes. Just as the bad news came with a phone call, the same phone can ring again with the answers, the miracle, the news that puts a smile on your face and a dance in your feet to make you spin around the room with delight. Relaxing in the face of bad news, a stressful day, or perplexing circumstances is a choice that you can make.

Yes, you may have bad moments or a bad day. But you have not lost the power to decide your response. Choose to chill.

CHANGE CHANNELS

Do not conform any longer to the pattern of this world, but be transformed by the renewing of your mind. Then you will be able to test and approve what God's will is—his good, pleasing and perfect will.

ROMANS 12:2

Only he who keeps his eye fixed on the far horizon will find his right road.

DAG HAMMARSKJÖLD

Watching what you feed your mind is equally as important, if not more so, than what you feed your body. Programs you watch on television, news reports you listen to, books you read, and conversations you entertain all affect you. What you allow to permeate your consciousness influences how you perceive and react to the world. Which is to say that looking at the world through eyes of Love—the law of Christ's kingdom—is how you can experience what the Scriptures seek to teach you.

Do you want to change your outlook? Good. Then change

your mind. Renew your mind by controlling what it feeds upon. If you want to see peace, you must look for it—must lay hold of it by surrounding yourself with persons, places, and things that represent it. If love is your goal, then you must seek it. Try reading books that fill your mind with thoughts of peace, love, harmony, and joy. Let the Word of God dwell richly in your heart; bathe your mind and thoughts by frequently meditating in His Scriptures and notice how you begin to see a new and more beautiful world.

Look at Jesus. He is our role model. Although he walked among a very unsettled generation—one filled with violence, anger, destruction, and fear—He is nonetheless called the Prince of Peace. If we take him as our example, it is then possible for us to live in these current turbulent times and still keep our peace, by keeping our thoughts, sights, and hearing on whatever strengthens and enriches us.

If you find yourself becoming agitated with life, check which station you are tuned in to. You may need to make an adjustment. Change channels!

THE BALL IS IN YOUR COURT

But when you pray, go into your room, close the door and pray to your Father, who is unseen. Then your Father, who sees what is done in secret, will reward you.

MATTHEW 6:6

To know how to live is my trade and my art.

MARCUS AURELIUS

One of my missions in performing my job responsibilities is to "get the ball out of my court." That technique serves me well and keeps me on course as I constantly strive to do what is required of me in order to meet the many deadlines that are an everyday part of my job. Obviously, when the ball is out of my court, I am relieved of my duties and can wait to see what is returned to me before taking further action.

Praying is similar to this. It is a way to cast your concerns off yourself and onto God. Remember, you are admonished to be anxious for nothing, "but in everything, by prayer and petition, with thanksgiving, present your requests to God" (Phil. 4:6).

When you pray, you are getting the ball out of this earthly court and into the realm of heaven. Once it is there, you can give thanks and relax. Your work is done. You need only to wait for the answer to be returned.

As you rise each day to greet new challenges, new requests, and new responsibilities, remember that by praying about everything, you are getting those cares and concerns off your spiritual shoulders and into God's arena. Confident of a response, you can then glance heavenward and whisper softly, "Hey, God! Ball's in your court!"

9·1·1

In all their distress he too was distressed, and the angel of his presence saved them. In his love and mercy he redeemed them; he lifted them up and carried them all the days of old.

ISAIAH 63:9

It's not the load that breaks you down, it's the way you carry it.

LENA HORNE

For each of us there is a place, a struggle, a trial where life knocks us to our knees. When you come to that place and find yourself completely out of strength, your very soul bowed over from much praying and void of hope, don't despair. You are now in a place where you can access one of the strongest, most faithful and eternal, attributes of God. It is His mercy.

Just when the heart faints, there is mercy. At that very point during your longest, hardest trial, there stands mercy. When you have tried everything to help yourself, prayed everything you can pray, cried every tear you can shed, strong and silent mercy is on standby, ready to carry you away into a place divinely reserved for you. Mercy is what remains to offer hope, strength, and ultimately deliverance. It is for those situations in which you say, "If God doesn't deliver me, I will perish."

Mercy is for that 9-1-1 situation you face. It is help for that unbearable situation. Even in a lengthy, seemingly unending, crisis, the God who is rich in mercy is able to rush in with divine life support to assist you in your miserable condition. Because you have long lain in suffering does not mean you will not be delivered.

Cry mercy for every emergency in your life. With invisible, flashing lights from heaven and the silent alarm of sirens, mercy will come swiftly to your rescue.

The Mountain Climber

And Jesus answering saith unto them, Have faith in God.

MARK 11:22 (KJV)

Be good at "letting go."

MARSHA SINETAR

They tell the story of a mountain climber who, desperate to conquer the Aconcagua in Argentina, finally initiated his climb after years of preparation. But he wanted the glory for himself and therefore went up alone. He started climbing and ascended for many hours. The hour become late. He hadn't prepared for camping and decided to keep on going. Soon it got dark . . .

Night fell with heaviness at a very high altitude. Visibility was zero. Everything was black. There was no moon, and the stars were covered by clouds. As he was climbing a ridge about one hundred meters from the top, he slipped and fell. Falling rapidly, he could only see blotches of darkness that passed quickly. He felt the terrible sensation of being sucked downward by gravity. He kept falling . . . and in those anguished moments good and bad memories passed through his mind. He thought he would certainly die.

But then he felt a jolt that almost tore him in half. Yes! Like any good mountain climber, he had staked himself with a long rope tied to his waist.

In those moments of stillness, suspended in the air, he had no other choice but to shout, "Help me, God! Help me."

All of a sudden he heard a deep voice from heaven. "What do you want me to do?"

"*Save me!*"

"Do you really think I can save you?"

"Of course, my God."

"Then cut the rope that is holding you up."

There was silence and stillness. The man just held tighter to the rope . . .

The rescue team says that the next day they found him, a frozen mountain climber hanging tightly to a rope . . . *two feet off the ground!*

How about you? How trusting are you in that rope? In God? Would you let go? I tell you God has great and marvelous things for you. Cut the rope and simply trust in Him.

VIRTUES

Do Good

Do not be overcome by evil, but overcome evil with good.

ROMANS 12:21

The only thing necessary for the triumph of evil is for good men to do nothing.

EDWARD BURKE

I was leaving from an afternoon visit with my mother, who suffered from Alzheimer's, when she softly said, "Do good." I was astonished. I had not heard her say those words since I was a young girl running up and down narrow, leaf-strewn paths in the hills of West Virginia.

In our household, to do good meant to do the very best you could. We were taught to put our best foot forward. We practiced this in every aspect of our lives—including our relationships. My mother knew we were put on this earth to help each other. She was an enlightened lady who knew that her life was like a handkerchief in her hand, and that with a mere wave of it she could influence her atmosphere, her lifestyle, and her destiny, simply by doing good. She sought by example to teach us this. It is a lesson I still strive to practice every day.

When we make a habit out of doing good, the result is phenomenal. What a wonderful opportunity and a unique way to weaken our adversarial forces. What a simple way!

Notice as you move through your day the ways in which you can do something good for someone else. Do you know of a woman who is going through a divorce? Why not send her a card to let her know you are praying for her. Have you been planning on complimenting someone on a new outfit? Do it!

I remember working with a lady who turned from her desk one day and said to me, "I am annoyed with you for not saying anything about my getting my hair done." I was utterly shocked. With complete honesty, I responded, "Honey, I never even noticed; your hair looks so good every day."

You can never tell the stress and struggles others are going through. Your smallest kindness might mean a great deal to them—might be just the thing they needed to get through the day. Don't miss your opportunity to do good. As women of the Word, may we be found always overcoming the negative with the good.

Develop Your Destiny

For as he thinketh in his heart, so is he.

PROVERBS 23:7 (KJV)

Never mention the word "failure." Always accentuate the positive.

EARL WOODS

Our parents never talked to us about the concept of defeat. To them it did not exist. These were two people raised in the Deep South who knew prejudice firsthand but refused to bow to its hand or magnify its influence in our lives. We were not to allow discrimination or inequality to be a determining factor in our success or upward mobility. In our minds, we were not unequal.

In our tiny, extremely humble, nine-hundred-square-foot home, our loving parents displayed attitudes that breathed with character, quality, and high aspirations. Ours was a land of extremes. To look at our possessions, we were very poor. But what lived unseen was the spirit of greatness my parents were developing in each of their children. Their very existence seemed riveted on instilling within us the desire to succeed—to believe in ourselves. They succeeded.

You can cultivate your own spirit of greatness. Bathe your mind in books that enrich and edify; surround yourself with positive people and teaching. Read often God's Word and think God thoughts. It will give you a bridge to walk on as you cross over from one lifestyle into another.

What is it you would like to achieve? Keep your eyes on the prize and never give up. It is within your reach to attain your goal. We serve a great and mighty God and by believing that "nothing is impossible with God" (Luke 1:27), you will develop the courage and strength to stride into a glorious future and a magnificent destiny.

Act As If . . .

Dear children, let us not love with words or tongue but with actions and in truth.

1 JOHN 3:18

We become just by performing just actions, temperate by performing temperate actions, brave by performing brave actions.

ARISTOTLE

Have you ever been in a situation where you felt uncomfortable? As you know, it feels better to stay within your comfort zones. But there are occasions that require us to stretch out—to launch out into areas and among people and environments different from what we are accustomed to. Why not act as if you are comfortable. Why not assume whatever virtue is needed at the time. Acting as if something is, makes it so. This is a powerful and fun principle to practice.

The next time you need a special undergirding of strength or some kind of emotional support for a social occasion, act as if you already possess it . . . and you will. Jesus tells us that when we pray and believe that we have received, we will.

What you do is important. It is in your doing that you become. Changing your behavior changes your reality. In doing, you take possession. Act as if you are happy and you will be. Act as if you are sad and you will be.

How you behave determines your emotional state. Pretend to be sick long enough and you will eventually feel the symptoms of illness. In the same way, acting as if you are well and unafraid brings about the desired result. If you keep doing something long enough, it naturally becomes a part of you. Acts of kindness will make you kind. Acts of giving will make you generous.

Saint Teresa of Avila said, "Accustom yourself continually to make many acts of love, for they enkindle and melt the soul." Our actions unlock the unseen doors that liberate us to evolve into women of distinction.

So what are you waiting for? Act!

WORK IT!

For even when we were with you, we gave you this rule: "If a man will not work, he shall not eat." We hear that some among you are idle. They are not busy; they are busybodies. Such people we command and urge in the Lord Jesus Christ to settle down and earn the bread they eat.

2 THESSALONIANS 3:10-12

Work is dignity and caring and the foundation for life with meaning.

MARIAN WRIGHT EDELMAN

I watched my father, Ernest Sr., work two and three jobs at one time most of his life. Even after opening his own janitorial business, which did so well that he eventually hired forty-two employees, he kept a side job going. Never did I see my father miss work. My brothers and I never came home from school to find our daddy off work because he was sick.

After we started school, Momma began working, and she made it look like something wonderful to do. Neither did my mother miss work. At the end of her day, she would talk excitedly about her job. My siblings and I have strong work ethics as a result of watching both her and my father.

If you are privileged to have work, whether you like the position that you are currently in or not, do not speak out against your job. It is the tool God is using to bring food to your table and shelter over your head. Until you get the position you desire, continue to thank God for the life, health, and strength to perform daily. It is your privilege and right to work. Rejoice that no one can take that from you.

We live in a society that legally allows, encourages, and applauds the working woman. While it is your season to work, shine!

WHO CARES?

I looked on my right hand, and beheld, but there was no man that would know me: refuge failed me; no man cared for my soul.

PSALM 142:4-5 (KJV)

As far as I am concerned, the greatest suffering is to feel alone, unwanted, unloved. The greatest suffering is also having no one, forgetting what an intimate, truly human relationship is, not knowing what it means to be loved, not having family or friends.

MOTHER TERESA

Have you ever had a complete stranger make your day by sharing a conversation with you while you're out conducting business or running errands?

Doing what you can to acknowledge another is a seemingly small and insignificant thing to do. However, a tiny smile and a simple hello and inquiry about how another person is feeling are simple efforts that allow you to say you see the other person and recognize he or she is there. Showing you are aware of an individual through a greeting is a powerful act of kindness. The other person may be healed by your smile and transformed through your words.

Unfortunately, most of us are oblivious to everything that is not a part of our little world and often don't take the time to express even the smallest of pleasantries. We are far too self-absorbed. This has the effect of making people feel invisible—a selfish and inconsiderate act. Everyone is deserving of our respect. However marred you and I and others may be, we are all made in the image of God and we ought to honor each person's journey through this earth. We don't have to do anything great to bless others. A simple hello will do.

Practicing the art of warmly acknowledging another soul holds the possibility of depositing limitless treasures into a life—yours and theirs.

What Do You Think?

Finally . . . whatsoever things are true, whatsoever things are honest, whatsoever things are just, whatsoever things are pure, whatsoever things are lovely, whatsoever things are of good report; if there be any virtue, and if there be any praise, think on these things.

PHILIPPIANS 4:8 (KJV)

Think of all the beauty still left around you and be happy.

ANNE FRANK

How you think determines your attitude and your outlook. What you think about shows up in your speech and ultimately in your actions. You reap the reward of a peaceable life when you make the effort to monitor your thoughts. If a thought isn't honest, virtuous, lovely, or positive, you should not entertain it.

Yet how often do you sit and ponder the six o'clock news, an e-mail bulletin, or some other troublesome piece of information that disturbs the peace and pollutes your perception? Away with stinking thinking! Since no one controls your thoughts but you, think smartly. Your thought life is a kingdom under your dominion; you are unmonitored and uncontrolled. That's a lot of power. What you do with that power is completely up to you. I encourage you to use your strength constructively and for good.

Additionally, because your thinking shapes your vision, character, and persona, allow it to pave a lovely path on the road of life. Direct your thoughts to higher ground. Think pretty thoughts. Think lovable and adorable thoughts. Think kind and generous thoughts. Think right.

Go for it!

DON'T WAIT UNTIL THANKSGIVING

O give thanks to the Lord of lords:
for his mercy endureth for ever.
To him who alone doeth great wonders:
for his mercy endureth for ever.

PSALM 136:3-4 (KJV)

The bitterest tears shed over graves are for words left unsaid
and deeds left undone.

HARRIET BEECHER STOWE

It is difficult to sympathize with people who are unappreciative. Apathy is an unfortunate attitude in many folks. But people who survive life-threatening situations and illnesses don't relate well to indifference. In their minds, there is so much around to be grateful for that we shouldn't have to look for a reason or wait for a season to give thanks. We should simply do it, whenever and wherever, regardless of our situations.

I once heard a lady say that whenever she starts to complain and whine and basically show an overall unthankful attitude, it's as if she can hear the Lord say to her, "Okay, do you want to trade out?" Immediately she becomes thankful for her life and for those people with whom she is involved. She is made to realize she is much better off than many and needs to act appropriately.

Out of the exuberance of a grateful heart, you must generously give thanks every day—to God, to family, to friends, to each other. Don't wait until an earth-shattering wake-up call plummets your life into despair before you are able to have a crystal-clear understanding of how good you have it. Even if you already have troubles, even in your lowest state, be glad things are as well as they are. Because it is almost certain there are others in the world suffering much more than you. There are others who have less who are doing more.

A glimpse of how rugged life could be is reason enough to quickly tell God "Thank you."

THE GIFT OF A TEACHER

*The same came to Jesus by night, and said unto him, Rabbi,
we know that thou art a teacher come from God: for no man
can do these miracles that thou doest, except God be with him.*

JOHN 3:2

A ton of reading does not equal one good teacher.

CHINESE PROVERB

All throughout the New Testament you will find inquiries
made of Jesus the teacher. His knowledge and ability to instruct
and inform were readily recognized by the people of His day.
Today, teachers seem to have lost their position of notoriety and
honor. This is sad. They deserve much more.

Teachers are well versed in instruction. They are the ones with
the ability to bypass our flesh and reach into our minds with the
light of instruction. My mother was an educator and she used her
gift to teach her children first and then her classroom. She recognized her responsibility and the golden opportunity she had to
unlock the mysteries of the world and open the darkroom of the

mind. It was her delight to shed light and understanding and to provide a pathway for each of us and for her students.

If you are an educator, you are blessed with a chance to enlighten and liberate another individual. If you are a student who has stumbled into the classroom of a good teacher, you are standing in the presence of greatness; do not allow this moment to pass without gleaning whatever you can from his or her mind. If you are neither a teacher nor a student, but simply a parent or friend who wishes to help instill the gift of knowledge into a young mind, don't let your opportunity pass by. Without good teachers and wise instruction, who will lead the way?

You Will Never See the Sun by Looking Down

I will lift up mine eyes unto the hills, from whence cometh my help.

PSALM 121:1 (KJV)

Where there's a will, there's a way. If you provide the will, God will provide the way.

BEVERLY BAILEY HARVARD

Most of you are aware of the many injustices in this country. Frankly, I would be concerned about anyone who is not aware and who does not loathe those injustices. However, how you react is another matter. Injustice is no excuse for bad attitudes, crime, racism, or other demonstrations of self-hatred.

Why? I'm glad you asked. When you walk around with a chip on your shoulder and a negative and foul attitude in your heart, it does more harm than any unjust legal system ever could. When you are downtrodden in your spirit, outlook, attitude, and aspirations, you have given power to your oppressors and have clouded your view with darkness.

You will never see the sun by looking down. And you will never get up unless you look up. It takes strength to defy the odds, to prevail in spite of a continual onslaught of desperate events. The good thing is you don't have to rely on your own strength. As believers, we are more than conquerors. In our weakness, God's strength is made perfect, and so we must allow His strength to shine in our lives. Your critics will be stymied when you are found relentlessly prevailing against them.

Injustice is an unfortunate but normal part of our daily existence. How we deal with it is another. Embrace God's strength, throw off those negative responses, hold your head high, and take a good look at that bright, shining sun above you!

A Song of Silence

The fruit of righteousness will be peace; the effect of righteousness will be quietness and confidence forever.

ISAIAH 32:17

The first requirement for prayer is silence. People of prayer are people of silence.

MOTHER TERESA

How easy it is to speak too quickly—to utter remarks better left unsaid. Our freedom of speech is contaminated daily through dangerous dialog. Many were the times my mother would warn me to not say everything I was thinking. I'm forever grateful she did.

What a mighty force silence is. The very absence of clutter in our minds and surroundings brings refreshment. Prayer time is a perfect way to experience this. It is a rewarding practice to steal away from the world for a quiet time that does the mind, body, and soul wonders. When we are freed from the noise of empty words constantly hurled at us and spoken by us, we are able to hear more distinctly what God would have us do and to envision more clearly the direction in which our lives should flow. Our ability to reflect, to evaluate, and to see becomes like the panoramic view inside a movie theater. Our ability to discern is more keen when our lives are not filled with aimless chatter.

In quietude, silence provides us a calmness, a supernatural sedative. When our spirits are thus sedated, through meditation and the study of the Word of God, we obtain the strength our lives so adamantly require and the blessed assurance we so desperately need.

"In quietness and in confidence shall be your strength" (Isa. 30:15 KJV). Embrace it!

Relish the Moments,
Cherish the Times

Why should any living man complain when punished for his sins? Let us examine our ways and test them, and let us return to the Lord.

LAMENTATIONS 3:39-40

Life was meant to be lived, and curiosity must be kept alive. One must never, for whatever reason, turn his back on life.

ELEANOR ROOSEVELT

Every day is a good day for a new resolution. We can start to better our lives at any time—at any point a new revelation hits us. If you discover some brilliant and wonderful truth, hurry and walk in it.

Making good use of your time is a good place to start. One of the wonderful aspects of aging is the certainty that you now have less time in front of you than what is behind. That's good enough reason to make every moment as satisfying as you possibly can, perform every kind and good deed you have ever considered, and simply spread as much joy and happiness around as you are able.

Youth embraces the deception that we will live forever. Middle-aged and older souls know better. We know every day is just one more excuse to celebrate life to the fullest. Each day is a present waiting for us to unwrap and share its precious contents with another. Our lives are sun-washed with treasures.

Use the good china every day. Wear that special outfit now. Go to that movie you keep saying you want to see. Better yet, call a friend to tag along. Make the phone call to that person who has been on your mind. Send that special gift without waiting for a birthday or a holiday. Give those loving words that you have been saving for just the right occasion.

Make your presence known on this earth by becoming a shining example of one who lifts other souls—by loving, giving, and sharing. Make as many people as you can glad you passed this way, not regretting the day you will pass away. You can start this moment to make yourself genuinely missed and dearly remembered by living your life today as if there will be no tomorrow.

Keeping It Real

Did not I weep for him that was in trouble? Was not my soul grieved for the poor?

JOB 30:25 (KJV)

Make the most of yourself, for that is all there is for you.

RALPH WALDO EMERSON

At one time or another most of us, usually from habit, complain and whine about the small aggravations of life. Like a window clouded from condensation formed on its pane, our perceptions are sometimes muddied by small inconveniences. Our spiritual eyesight has momentarily lost insight into what really matters.

To keep your perspective free from contamination, try weighing your life on the scales of authenticity. Petty annoyances and inconsequential nuisances hardly constitute real trouble. A real problem is something that cannot be humanly fixed. Real poverty is not about having enough money to buy food for supper tonight. A real problem is no food to eat for days and weeks and no idea as to when you will ever eat again.

Listen to folks in a long grocery line as offenses are uttered to the clerks—all while standing in an air-conditioned building filled with enough food to feed a small country somewhere on this planet. Or watch people honking their horns from air-conditioned cars during a traffic jam as they slowly creep past others walking to and from sweltering bus stops during a heat wave.

The next time you encounter a petty annoyance, I challenge you to remember that the very fact that you are inconvenienced means that you are also very privileged. The temporary loss of what we feel is due us is a gentle reminder to pray for others less fortunate. It is also an opportunity to uproot from our lives any arrogance that seeks to creep in like weeds in an abandoned field—keeping it from taking over space more suitable for expanding some rare treasure that may lie hidden within us.

GET INTO PRACTICE

Whatever you have learned or received or heard from me, or seen in me—put it into practice. And the God of peace will be with you.

PHILIPPIANS 4:9

Success is the sum of small efforts, repeated day in and day out.

ROBERT COLLIER

Are we, as citizens of this earthly realm and future citizens of Christ's heavenly kingdom, supposed to sit and wait for something or someone to help us change our bad habits and behaviors? No. Christ clearly said to put into practice what he taught. You and I should be always accustomed to doing good deeds and other kindnesses. Virtues are practiced, not waited upon. Prayed for, nor meditated about. They are acted out.

Now is the time to put your money where your mouth is, as they say, and to become accustomed to walking in a manner that will be your eternal role. Christ said it is the wise man who hears His words and puts them into practice (Matt. 7:24). You need to rehearse now, before it's too late and you find yourself standing awkwardly in front of heavenly cameras, staring into the brightest of all lights, a foreigner to virtues that should be second nature to you.

Wise women are prepared. A wonderful lady I know lives her life with the motto "To love." I have never sat and talked with her that she did not demonstrate love and concern. Once, while chatting with her on the phone, I shared with her my attraction to peace and silence and she shared with me her strong captivation with love. Her ability to love and to exude love to everyone she encounters has so impacted me that watching her love makes me want to love, too. From that conversation, I began to realize the significance of pouring love into and from every area of life. What she has put into practice has become a part of her.

Victorious living comes through practice. Are you ready?

You Big Phony!

Therefore I urge you to imitate me.

1 CORINTHIANS 4:16

One must learn by doing the thing; though you think you know it, you have no certainty until you try.

SOPHOCLES

Tell me, do you think it is ever okay to be phony? I don't either. We are encouraged to imitate what is good, not what is fake. We are told to imitate Christ. As Christians we are known by our character—if we have Christlike traits, we are successfully following in the footsteps of our Lord.

The apostle Paul said to follow him as he followed Christ. Jesus said for us to take up our cross and follow Him. What Christ did was to go about doing good. Today, as you follow His instructions, try to duplicate His efforts and emulate His behavior. As you dwell in His Word and do the same deeds He performed—feed the poor, clothe the naked, visit the sick and incarcerated—you will be imitating the Master.

What will keep you, who follows the Light of the world, from being a counterfeit is your entitlement and permission to portray Him who dwells in you. Don't copy me, don't copy others, but instead imitate the Divine. As you do, you will look less like a phony and more like Him.

As followers of Christ, we are continually made into His image. That should ever be our desired end.

Time to Pay It Back

And the King shall answer and say unto them, Verily I say unto you, Inasmuch as ye have done it unto one of the least of these my brethren, ye have done it unto me.

MATTHEW 25:40 (KJV)

Service is the rent that you pay for room on this earth.

SHIRLEY CHISHOLM

We owe people. We owe our forefathers. We owe our grandparents. We owe our parents.

More than likely, most of your forebears have already passed out of your life and live now only in your past, and no more do you have the opportunity to recompense them. But that doesn't mean you can't pay off your debt in other ways. If you are unable to gift your ancestors, it's time for you to pass on something to your children, grandchildren, and other members of family and society. Going through life as if it is just about you—as if you owe no one—is a selfish, immature, and isolating way to think. Not to mention untruthful! You didn't get where you are completely on your own.

You and I are obligated to do whatever we can, wherever we can, to help others. It is our duty to be our brother's keeper. This can be in word, in deed, in money—in many varied ways. Donate your time to a volunteer cause. Make a monetary donation to an organization in the name of your parents. Make cookies for a school bake sale for your kids. There are so many things you can do.

Sharing what we have with others doesn't diminish our worth. It multiplies and enlarges our souls.

Making Happy

Instead, it should be that of your inner self, the unfading beauty of a gentle and quiet spirit, which is of great worth in God's sight.

1 Peter 3:4

Happiness depends, as nature shows, less on exterior things than most suppose.

William Cowper

It sounds incredibly simple to say, but many of the decisions regarding the emotional state of our existence are placed into our own hands. Simply making concrete determinations on how we will respond to each circumstance is one key. Beyond that, by simply focusing our attention on the little things we come to see what matters greatly.

Sound trivial? Not so! Little things, such as sunshine pouring through the window each morning and the feel of its warmth on our feet where they touch the sunny floor, have a great influence on our lives. The mere application of looking for tiny, obscure pleasures can increase our ability to "make happy" almost anywhere, anytime, anyplace. Noticing the freshness of the air, the smell of the earth, or the brightness of the sky can literally make the difference in whether you have a good, bad, or mediocre day.

The ability to appreciate the beauty of everyday ordinary things like billowy clouds in the morning sky, insects buzzing by, and the ebb and flow of life from day to day is the beginning of training oneself to see the larger picture—to see the loveliness in one another. When we can derive pleasure from the soundless throb of life, so apparent in front of our faces, ultimately our trained eyes will more easily recognize the "unfading beauty of a gentle and quiet spirit" that Peter admonishes each woman to possess.

Stop being oblivious to all the joy around you. Develop a razor-sharp sensor for what is lovely and pure. Then you will indeed be able to look behind the veil of flesh and behold the inner beauty in another's soul—its quiet inner beauty. Because you have seen, appreciated, and applauded the beauty of nature and readily enjoy the imperceptible qualities that many others may miss, the shimmering quality of a rich soul will not escape you. That kind of ability is a gift to be treasured, cultivated, and shared.

So, wake up!

Give Honor Where Honor Is Due

Give everyone what you owe . . . if respect, then respect; if honor, then honor.

ROMANS 13:7

Life is just a short walk from the cradle to the grave, and it sure behooves us to be kind to one another along the way.

ALICE CHILDRESS

During the course of a very large women's meeting, I passed by a lady wearing a beautiful necklace and bracelet. I stopped briefly to compliment her on the beautiful jewelry and moved on. Midway through the meeting, I passed by the same lady again and she stopped me, gently reached for my hand, and pressed into it the jewelry I had earlier praised. The woman had been so appreciative of my compliment that she gave the object of my attention to me. She insisted I take it, and so I did. I was humbled and flattered.

How many times do we see a sister dressed to the nines and pass by her without the slightest indication that we noticed the time she took to present herself so beautifully? Why are we so quick to praise God and so stingy with our tributes to one another? Our praise and adoration of God, whom we cannot see, is questionable if we cannot acknowledge the lady sitting next to us. Would we not be offended if that same woman didn't clean herself up and dress appropriately? I'm sure a lot of gossiping would soon ensue if she were publicly unbecoming. And yet, we have not a word for the woman who prepares herself as though for her king.

The next time you see your coworker or neighbor or the lady in your church, sorority, or club looking especially nice, at the very least nod or smile your approval. Or, do something completely outrageous and tell her she looks exquisite! Your act of kindness may make a difference in her life and her attitude. It will certainly enlarge you as an individual.

Who knows, she might even give you the outfit, too!

I Got It!

Enter into his gates with thanksgiving, and into his courts with praise: be thankful unto him, and bless his name.

PSALM 100:4 (KJV)

I thank you. I am not of many words, but I thank you.

WILLIAM SHAKESPEARE

On a very rare occasion, some of us might forget to say thank you, but it should certainly be the exception rather than the rule.

Telling each other and our God thank you is vitally important. Not only is it our way of expressing our gratitude for some deed, it is an absolute response that ensures the giver that we received whatever was sent to us. We are not just being polite and considerate; we are acknowledging that we have been the recipient of an act or an item.

Recently, I mailed some items to a lady across the country. Since she did not know I was sending the gifts, I phoned after nearly six weeks of not having heard anything from her. Perhaps, I thought, she has moved, or the package was lost in the mail, or even sent to an incorrect address. What I found was that the package had indeed arrived. The recipient simply hadn't told me.

Acknowledging a gift or deed by saying thank you shows appreciation. In the book of Luke, we find Jesus amazed that after healing ten lepers, only one of them bothered to return to say thank you and to glorify God (Luke 17:12-19). It is important that we thank one another, but it is imperative that we thank and glorify God. It is the only way to communicate that we appreciate the heavenly attention.

The next time you are blessed to receive, be sure to say "Thank you." If not, heaven may withhold its generous hand the next time around, waiting to hear a response from your last request!

DON'T WRITE ME OFF!

May the God who gives endurance and encouragement give you a spirit of unity among yourselves as you follow Christ Jesus, so that with one heart and mouth you may glorify the God and Father of our Lord Jesus Christ. Accept one another, then, just as Christ accepted you, in order to bring praise to God.

ROMANS 15:5-7

Patience is bitter, but its fruit is sweet.

FRENCH PROVERB

In order for us to fulfill the Word of God, we must sometimes practice (or even pretend!) tolerance for and acceptance of one another, until what we have acted out becomes a natural part of our repertoire. If you can stand with me when you can't stand me and if you will strive to overlook my faults and flaws, we have a much better chance of surviving our differences and coming into a place of unity and affection for one another, which is God's ultimate goal.

Believe me, I'm doing the same thing. If I wrote off everyone who annoyed me or who simply didn't appeal to me, there wouldn't be anyone left! But no one wants to be alone at the end of their life. You don't, do you? A sure way to live an empty and unfulfilled existence is to not be able to stand anyone but yourself. Something is very wrong with that.

Finding something in common with another individual is the easiest way to bridge the gap and to forget our differences. I remember many years ago working with a lady with a background very dissimilar from mine. It was obvious she had not had much exposure to people of other races. Rather than becoming intolerant of her lack of cultural exposure, I noticed that we shared a like passion for a particular craft. As we began to interact around our common interest, a friendship developed.

If you give others the benefit of the doubt, you might find a future friend or at least a pleasant acquaintance. Take a moment and contemplate life. I think it will become increasingly clear to you that we need each other in this world. Things, articles, and objects are not going to console you in this world. The only contentment you will find will be through other people.

Start today . . .

WISHFUL THINKING

Resentment kills a fool, and envy slays the simple.

JOB 5:2

Everybody must learn this lesson somewhere—that it costs something to be what you are.

SHIRLEY ABBOTT

For some reason, especially in the United States, we seem to look at one another and assume the other possesses wholeness. We seem to think the other person has got it all together, and when we view their possessions and lifestyle, we inwardly covet what does not belong to us. Somehow we have incorporated a lot of contaminated information into our spirits and we believe the grass really is greener on the other side of the fence. The truth is this is dangerous thinking.

Never ask for someone's existence, lifestyle, or possessions. It costs them something to be whoever they are, just as it costs you to be who you are. Besides that, what you may see with your eye is only a small portion of what is really going on in that person's life. Our soft, silky skins are akin to coarse, dense walls—they hide what is really going on inside of us.

I remember many years ago watching a popular Christian television program and listening to a woman being interviewed who had suffered a stroke. The announcer beamed at the lovely lady and said how she looked as if she had never suffered a malady. To which she replied, "I look better than I feel." Although no one had been able to tell, she didn't quite feel on the inside how she looked on the outside.

Everything that glitters is not gold. Appearances are deceiving. Before you longingly aspire to be like someone successful who appears outwardly blessed and popular, steady yourself and calm your thoughts. You might be shocked to find out how much better your life is than the person's you are seeking to emulate.

Women who are envious or jealous waste precious energy wishing for things they think would make their lives better when instead they could be expending precious energy on developing their full potential. Be grateful for who you are, wherever you are, no matter what you are going through. God made you for a reason!

SPINNING STRAW INTO GOLD

Those who sow in tears will reap with songs of joy.

PSALM 126:5

Women whose eyes have been washed clear with tears get broad vision.

DOROTHY DIX

It's all too easy, in the whole scheme of life, to become internally lost in the maze of events and circumstances that daily shape, distract, and involve us. Life pulls at us. It stretches us and pokes us and leaves us not the same as we were before. We might naturally assume this is a bad thing. But sometimes on our journey, what we perceive as the painful, natural progression of life—down-and-dirty living—is the very thing that ultimately makes us the beautiful, colorful patchwork that is ourself.

Why do we dismiss the obvious? Why do we continually doubt that, as the Bible states, the trials of life are what shape us and make us stronger (1 Pet. 5:10)? The most beautiful sunsets come from air pollution. The best fruits and vegetables are grown in manure. The greatest opportunity for blessing is in the lives of the most afflicted.

When you see the struggles, the oppression, the hindrances of life as the very ingredients that will make you flower into a world-class woman, then you will know the power of all things working together for your good. Then you will be able to embrace your struggles and make something of them—make something of yourself. Now is your opportunity to grow emotionally and spiritually. Now is your opportunity to allow the fires of life to strengthen you in their kiln. You will emerge a better person for it.

You have been given a pile of straw? Well, what are you waiting for? Now, spin!

SALTY LADY

Salt is good, but if it loses its saltiness, how can you make it salty again? Have salt in yourselves, and be at peace with each other.

MARK 9:50

You must be the change you wish to see in the world.

MAHATMA GANDHI

In the midst of coping with the pressures of daily living, stop and consider that you have the substance, the stuff, to live and to live well. We are the salt of this earth, sprinkled lavishly into diverse settings of human experience specifically to add flavor to life and to enrich our earthly journey with blessings.

So you think you don't make a difference? Think again. You and I carry within us the zest of living, and it pours out of us and into our environment. Silent as salt, we affect everything we encounter. We touch each other's hopes and dreams with our expressions, our responses, and our presence. You are leaving a savory, lasting impression and distinctive flavoring in whatever or whomever you come into contact with.

You have the opportunity to scatter blessings throughout this world as seasoning for others' souls. Without words, you can bring life to bland and dull situations while scrubbing away dead things with your salty behavior. Grain by grain, take the time to add just enough flavor to bring out the good in people's lives with the condiments of enthusiasm and excitement necessary to revive the fainting soul.

It is your zeal for living that is contagious, and others will extract refreshment from it to enliven and preserve their own existence.

ROOTS

By *wisdom a house is built, and through understanding it is established.*

PROVERBS 24:3

Where there is great love there are always miracles.

WILLA CATHER

You and I may never take the time to trace our heritage, but if you were fortunate enough to have good parenting, you should consider the impact your parents made on your life. I hope you had someone—a parent, an aunt, a grandmother, a concerned teacher or pastor—speak treasures into your life.

Good parenting is the infrastructure that affects us indefinitely. My parents were heavily involved in our lives. My two brothers and I were not allowed to aimlessly wander about without mental, emotional, and spiritual supervision. We were provided an invisible road map to help guide us through this life. Life lessons were given by our mother to show us how to think—how to make wise decisions and to know the difference between right and wrong. I realize how blessed I was to have such an upbringing and I never want to take it for granted.

If the ground you stand on is shaky because your childhood was void of guidance, think often on the wonderful words of the old hymn, "On Christ the solid rock I stand, all other ground is sinking sand." Whatever wisdom and training you did not receive from your earthly parents, you have the opportunity to receive instruction from your heavenly Father. We have the sure and magnificent blessing of an amazing spiritual family tree. Its history is recorded in God's Word. Take advantage of it!

I Had the Power

A cheerful heart is good medicine.

PROVERBS 17:22

Strength is a matter of the made up mind.

JOHN BEECHER

I love to laugh. But you and I both know life is not always funny. Did you know that your ability to extract joy and happiness from a challenging world is a gift? I did not discover the power of laughter until I lay flat on my back in a hospital bed listening to my oldest brother, Ernest, tell funny stories to make me laugh.

God does you a favor when He allows you to fill your mouth with laughter. Your ability to grin, giggle, and guffaw is not only a release, it is a power tool. When you laugh, discouragement, darkness, and despair flee. Some women cleanse their souls with tears. But I prefer laughter. Bubbly gusts of exuberant laughter softly sandblast the soul, ridding you of contaminants that seek to pollute. It's a method of detoxification.

The freedom to laugh also reveals a trust in God that says you believe everything to be alright in your life—or at least that you will be able to overcome. A merry heart shows your confidence in the Creator. Our willingness to demonstrate merriment or joy is a signal to God that we trust Him for all things. It is a sign of our faith in Him. It is the reason we are told to praise the Lord—in all things. Boldly, powerfully, we are making the statement through our actions that we are victorious. Our uncommon display of trust in God even provides a road for Him to send answers to prayer. We exercise hilarious faith!

Today I challenge you to laugh—to open wide your heart and your arms and to giggle with gusto. If someone says something hurtful, laugh. If the car won't start, laugh. If you're tired and still have four hours of work to go, laugh. If the children are squabbling and your husband wants to know where dinner is, by all means laugh! And know that God is sovereign and ever present in your life.

Go ahead. Laugh!

But for a Moment

And God said, "Let there be lights in the expanse of the sky to separate the day from the night, and let them serve as signs to mark seasons and days and years."

GENESIS 1:14

If we take care of the moments, the years will take care of themselves.

MARIA EDGEWORTH

I know we are urged to have life plans—to know where we will be in our careers, marriages, and goals ten years from now. But there is something to be said for greeting each day with fresh enthusiasm and with the pure, untouched hope of simply accomplishing our goals for this morning, this afternoon, and the hours before we go to bed.

Moment by moment you move through this day, this week, this month, this year, this life. Deciding what you will do with each instant is far more manageable than trying to live out your existence in immense blocks of time. Of course you should plan for the future. But only with the knowledge that eternity is played out in your life moment by moment. Slowing down to grasp that truth will allow you the freedom and ability to make wise choices and sound decisions.

Our society applauds people who are multitasked, but there is such more accomplished and enjoyed when tasks are done one at a time. When we live scattered lives, hitting at this and aiming at that, we are doing a lot, but we may not be experiencing or savoring much of anything. Living in the present moment keeps us focused on the task at hand and away from wondering and worrying about the future or regretting the past.

We must slow down. Line upon line, precept upon precept, a little at a time, moves us through one day at a time. You may be feeling totally bombarded right now with many tasks to complete, but remember that even God sliced infinity into time that we might have order and structure through the seasons, years, and days. Ultimately, the present time is all that we have.

Carefully creating our future by the moment, we are giving ourselves the liberty to enjoy our days.

It Is Well

Therefore do not worry about tomorrow, for tomorrow will
worry about itself. Each day has enough trouble of its own.

MATTHEW 6:34

Worry is like racing the engine of an automobile without letting in the clutch.

CORRIE TEN BOOM

Nothing I have ever been through has left me without the presence of God or stripped me of His counsel. Nothing has ever sep-
arated me from Him. No matter what state I have been reduced
to, no matter what has stricken me, I have never been without
the ability to enter His presence.

You would do well to remember this important lesson: even at
your lowest point, when the worst has come to pass, God is there.
He is closer to you than the breath in your mouth. He is so much
a part of you that it is an impossibility to divide one from the
other.

So why do you insist upon worrying? Come on, I know you do!

We all do. We women spend a great deal of time worrying about things that never come to pass. We waste hours, days, weeks, and years fearing events during which, if they ever do occur, we still look up to find God by our side, faithful to the end. He has always been so. Scriptures record instance upon instance of God's enduring faithfulness.

Therefore, if God is never going to leave us—and He won't— then we might as well look our troubles in the eye and with a toss of our confident head say with lightheartedness, "It is well with me. Because there is nowhere that He is not, and no matter what occurs He will be with me throughout."

You and I have seen too many victories to continue the bad habit of worry. Go on, my friend. Step forth in confidence. He is there. He is faithful. It is well.

First, Do No Harm

Do not touch my anointed ones; do my prophets no harm.

1 Chronicles 16:22

To heal divisions, to relieve th' opprest; in virtue rich; in blessing others, blest.

Alexander Pope

My mother once said, "When raising children it is not necessary to win every battle; it is far more important to win the war." Her goal was to build and shape whole children without doing irreversible damage that would linger long into our futures.

Sadly, so much of today's teaching encourages us to win and to win at all costs, irrespective of the injury and damage suffered by our opponents, families, and friends. These destructive modes of manipulation sear the soul and totally obstruct loving, wholesome thinking and behavior. We must awake to the value of handling one another with care, mindful that we are to refrain from doing wrongful things to each other, seeking at the very least not to inflict upon each other undue or unnecessary pain.

Ladies, we have a natural sense of beauty about us. It is because we are caretakers. We kiss the boo-boos on our children's scraped knees. We softly whisper encouraging words into the ears of our men. We underpin our sons and daughters with consoling words and statements that strengthen. We talk long into the night to encourage our friends. Today, remember to raise your gaze and look for every opportunity to lift some wounded maiden, some bended soul, up and into the marvelous healing light.

EAT IT!

Endure hardship with us like a good soldier of Christ Jesus.

2 TIMOTHY 2:3

It doesn't matter what you're trying to accomplish, it's all a matter of discipline . . . I was determined to discover what life held for me beyond the inner-city streets.

WILMA RUDOLPH

I grew up in a family where dinner was served on a small, rusty-legged Formica table in the middle of a tiny kitchen at a specific hour each day. Every family member showed up at the dinner table, grace was said, and we sat down to eat whatever our momma had prepared.

Now Momma had a knack for budgeting and she stretched her grocery money by fixing us affordable and nutritious food. Turnip bottoms were one of her favorite things to feed us. To this day, I cannot stand the smell of cooking turnip bottoms. Needless to say, my mother was not interested in what I thought of her menu, and my brothers and I were made to eat everything on our plates.

What I did not know then was that although what Momma prepared may not have been tasty to me, it was nutritious. It may not have been my choice of foods to eat, but it was doing great things for my body, turnip bottoms and all.

It is the same with life. Sometimes life will serve you situations, people, environments, and challenges that do not appeal to your appetite. You are nevertheless put in a position where you have to take it in anyway. You have to keep things in perspective and remember that consuming things you don't like is probably doing more good for you than what you initially see. Perhaps the pink slip at the job is preparing you for something better. Perhaps those trials at home are honing you for future events. Perhaps the tensions between you and a friend will make your bond stronger in the end.

As you bear the unpleasantries of this world, consider that what you undergo may be the very things that will make you stronger, more resilient, and more able to endure your journey through this world. So, take a deep breath, hold your nose, and . . . eat it!

WOUNDED WARRIOR

For my strength is made perfect in weakness. Most gladly therefore will I rather glory in my infirmities, that the power of Christ may rest upon me.

2 CORINTHIANS 12:9 (KJV)

Do not go where the path may lead, go instead where there is no path and leave a trail.

RALPH WALDO EMERSON

Have you considered using your adversity as your weapon? I just received an e-mail from a lady who had gotten a rather dismal medical diagnosis. She, like most of us would be, was afraid. As I wrote her encouraging words, I also wondered if she might consider using this time to become relentless.

What exactly do I mean? Our attitude and our outlook determine our successes as we confront what is hurled at us in this life. If perhaps you are going through some situation that is less than desirable, you have the choice to view it as a temporary assignment to the front lines and to use the struggle as a tool to blaze your way to victories and successes that you might not otherwise attempt. Your adversity is not your excuse. People who are wounded fight better than the nonchalant or apathetic. A wounded warrior becomes alert and crystal clear about what really matters. A wounded warrior pushes forward and becomes more focused and imaginative than folks who have fallen asleep at the dreary wheel of their humdrum and boring life. Wounded warriors see opportunities where others walk blind and oblivious. When we see our disadvantages as advantages and our low places as stepping stones, then, even in sufferings, you and I are victorious.

It was only after I had become ill that I became wide-eyed to the handlebars of hope, alive to the supernatural, and strong beyond measure in faith. I trust you will not have to go through anything like I did. But whatever your situation, I encourage you to have the right attitude.

Fight on.

❧

*...d with all your heart and lean not on your
Tr...nding.*
ow...

PROVERBS 3:5

...takes twenty years to become an overnight success.

EDDIE CANTOR

It takes supernatural strength to muster courage in the face of life's disappointments. When the relationship you invested so much hope, love, and time into fails, it is hard to dismiss it like dust particles falling from the soles of shoes. When that new job you so coveted ends up to be not what you expected, even the increase in income does not salve your disappointment.

It's difficult to act as if things that are important to you don't matter. They do. But how you react to disappointment is the key. Facing dissatisfactions and discouragement takes character. It also takes vision. In order to receive physical or emotional healing, you must be honest. You are not invincible; you can be hurt.

In fact, you most likely want to buck... ness when your plans are thwarted and

Momma used to say, "Every story doe... ing." This we know! So why do we always... when things don't go as we'd planned? Wh... things don't go as you plan? Do you stay positive... and enthusiastic in the face of obvious dissatisfact...

When the world is not as you'd wish, treat your ... disillusioned, frustrated, and unhappy self to as mu... and kindness as you can. Don't blame yourself for the ... of life. Now is a time to celebrate yourself as Queen for a... a week, a month, a summer, or a year). For as long as it ... reward yourself in the same ways you would nurture and con... a friend. Extinguish the flames of your despair and doubt wit... self-care, tenderness, love, and peace until you feel you have bol- stered your fragile and precious life.

You matter. You are valuable. Gently help yourself to get back up. You are still rising.

COURAGEMENT

Succeeding at Success

In everything he did he had great success, because the Lord was with him.

1 SAMUEL 18:14

Success can make you go one of two ways. It can make you a prima donna—or it can smooth the edges, take away the insecurities and let the nice things come out.

BARBARA WALTERS

Have you had a recent success or two? Surprised? Why?

Everyone wants to be successful at something. Our human need to achieve and our spiritual quest to master, to triumph and subdue, is intrinsic. Inherent within all of us abides the itch to be accomplished at one thing or another. And you and I won't stop scratching until we have won at something and prevailed over those goals we deem worthy to pursue.

I often find myself repeating my mother's words, "I don't understand people who don't want anything." Momma was a successful woman who knew the challenges of acquiring a degree, earning a position, winning a part in the town hall play, or arriving at a desired standard of living. Challenges shape and strengthen us and form us into fully developed women. From our mastery, we become women adept at handling our business.

There is no room for arrogance in this journey; our help comes from the Lord. By meditating in the Scriptures and skillfully applying the Word of God like medicine to wounds, we are met with triumph. The more success, the more our confidence and self-esteem climbs to unimaginable heights. We are released to journey to foreign places, unfamiliar areas, and uncharted territories to do mighty exploits. Amazingly, from the womb of one success, we find that we can produce multiple births. Our successes birth more success. With a domino effect, we find our lives evolving from glory to glory.

So I ask you, why are you surprised? You are merely reaping what you have sown. Congratulations!

Don't Settle

Make it your ambition to lead a quiet life, to mind your own business and to work with your hands, just as we told you, so that your daily life may win the respect of outsiders and so that you will not be dependent on anybody.

1 Thessalonians 4:11-12

You don't have to have fought in a war to love peace.

Geraldine Ferraro

We are here because someone else fought to survive and thrive to make this world a better place for you and me to live in. Don't settle for anything less. Too much has been given up for you to be here. Too many struggles. Too many wars. Too many battles have been won for us to not continue the pursuit of a more peaceful, responsible, loving society for our descendants.

You and I must rise from whatever level we are currently on for the good of those coming behind us. We have the responsibility to do well so that we can help someone else. It really is better to give than to receive. I'd rather hand you a one-hundred-dollar bill than need it myself.

Wouldn't you feel better paying someone else's rent than needing for yours to be paid? Wouldn't you prefer giving away your clothes, feeding the hungry, and praying for the oppressed, depressed, and discouraged than living in want? How can you be a blessing to someone else if you are always in need?

You should want more so that you can do more. For yourself and for other people, too.

I Missed My Opportunity!

[They] said to Moses, "We have become unclean because of a dead body, but why should we be kept from presenting the Lord's offering with the other Israelites at the appointed time?"

Moses answered them, "Wait until I find out what the Lord commands concerning you."

NUMBERS 9:7-8

I always had only one prayer: "Lord, just crack the door a little, and I'll kick it open all the way."

SHIRLEY CAESAR

In the Scripture above, the people panicked at the thought of a lost opportunity to celebrate the Lord's Passover. The likelihood of being able to participate was virtually impossible . . . until Moses sought the Lord on their behalf.

Sometimes we give up too easily in life. At the first sign of a roadblock, many of us prepare for a U-turn when in fact we should do like the Israelites in this passage and inquire. Most opportunities are made from our pursuing them. Sometimes relentlessly. Our very destiny is usually tied up in some challenge.

For example, if you have missed or neglected your opportunity to parent, do you have grandchildren? You now have the knowledge and grace to bless them—use it. Were you unable to have children? There are so many children waiting to be rescued. Adopt or foster one—or two! Did you not get the formal education you desired? Can you help someone else obtain their degree? Or are you even willing to start working on getting your own? Never got married? Hey, you're never "too old" to find someone!

I think you get my point. There really is no such thing as a lost opportunity. You may have been delayed, or detoured, but you cannot be denied.

Ask for What You Want

*So I say to you: Ask and it will be given to you . . . For every-
one who asks receives.*

LUKE 11:9-10

*The job is to ask questions and it always was and to ask them
as inexorably as I can. And to face the absence of precise
answers with a certain humility.*

ARTHUR MILLER

With the relentless fervor of a two-year-old, we with record-
breaking consistency make our prayer requests known unto God.
And we whine and cry when we think they have not been
answered—at least to our satisfaction. Why do we throw such silly
tantrums? Clearly the Scriptures tell us that those who ask, receive.
It is impossible for God to lie. So why do we feel so many prayers
go "unanswered"? Could the problem be in our receptivity?

Sometimes I think we are like the individual in the story who
was drowning and prayed for God to help. Shortly, a helicopter
flew low to rescue him, but the man said he was waiting on God.

A little later, as the man continued to pray, a boat patrol came by and threw a line out to the tired, dehydrated man. But again he refused, saying he was waiting on God. Several more unsuccessful rescue attempts were made on his behalf. Obviously this man drowned. In his mind, his prayers went unanswered.

Is it possible that our perception has become so impaired we do not recognize answered prayer? We must become like Elijah the prophet, who did not give up in prayer, but continued until what he had seen in his spirit was manifest outwardly. First Kings 18:44 says: "The seventh time the servant reported, 'A cloud as small as a man's hand is rising from the sea.' So Elijah said, 'Go and tell Ahab, Hitch up your chariot and go down before the rain stops you.' "

Elijah was praying for rain. Each time he prayed, his servant went out to check the skies. When the servant returned after the seventh time to report a cloud the size of a man's hand, Elijah recognized immediately the answer to his prayer. The cloud meant rain was imminent. He did not wait until the raindrop fell, but knew the cloud contained the rain he sought. He had faith.

Check to see what has appeared on the horizon of your life. It may be your answer to prayer. It may be temporarily hidden or even wrapped in personal struggles. But it's there. Train your eye to see what or who may be holding your answer. Think outside the box, as they say. And as you survey your surroundings, keep in mind that "everyone who asks receives."

Ask for what you want. Recognize it when it comes.

Watch Where You're Going!

All the land that you see I will give to you.

GENESIS 13:15

What we see depends mainly on what we look for.

SIR JOHN LUBBOCK

If you drive a vehicle, you already understand the principle of keeping your eyes on the road. Glancing at a distraction off to the side will usually cause you to move in the direction in which you are looking. And soon you find yourself meandering off the highway to places you hadn't intended going! Staying focused on the right object, the right view, the right direction keeps you moving toward your goal.

Making a practice of watching only the places you want to go in life—selective viewing—also helps you arrive at the desired destination. The next time you end up in a place or situation that surprises you, check to see where you have been looking. Have you become preoccupied with negative or unimportant things? If you don't want it in your life, stop staring at it. Instead, keep your gaze on the lookout for good and that's where you will end up. God told Abraham to look out over the land before him and that everything that Abraham saw was his (Gen. 17:8). Now that's a sight worth concentrating on!

Watch where you are going. And remember: if you look at the cornfield, you will surely drive off the road and into the field!

YOU WILL LAUGH AGAIN

For his anger lasts only a moment, but his favor lasts a life-time; weeping may remain for a night, but rejoicing comes in the morning.

PSALM 30:5

Flowers grow out of the dark moments.

CORITA KENT

Have faith in God, who holds your future. Despite the present darkness that you may be groping through, do not believe the sun will not shine again in your life. You will laugh again.

When your world has been assailed with life's savage realities, it's hard to believe that things will ever get better, that you will ever laugh, that all will be well with your world. But hold on and hold out. Step by step, one day at a time and moment by moment, normalcy, order, and even happiness will flood over you as if darkness had never been a great part of your life.

Darkness is deceiving. All things look different in the night. They look more frightening, more permanent, more threatening.

Remember, there are no permanent storms; either you rise above the storm or it ceases to rage in your life. Ultimately, we will all leave all our troubles behind.

I remember a pivotal moment in my own recovery process. Standing on the stairs of our tiny little home, I froze in my tracks. I had just put my only child, Kelly, to bed and had made some inane comment to her. Unimportant what was said, what happened was inconceivable: I laughed.

Our little house had not heard laughter for so many long months that its sound was shocking to me. To my child. To the walls. The carpet. Everything around me stood motionless in time, trying to understand what had just occurred and seeking to experience every second of the event. My memory gingerly turned the sound in every direction to inspect it. I became silent with wonder. Things had been so bad for such a long time, I had ceased to expect laughter. Nothing in my life was funny. Yet, it had happened. And from that day forward, little by little, joy returned to me.

You may have experienced the worst ordeal of your life. But keep walking. Keep moving. This too shall pass. You really will laugh again. Hidden behind the darkest night, crouched underneath the blackest despair, is laughter, waiting for the express moment that it can sneak, soft as a cloud, out of your worst nightmare and into your reality.

LADIES IN WAITING

My eyes will flow unceasingly, without relief, until the Lord looks down from heaven and sees. What I see brings grief to my soul because of all the women of my city.

LAMENTATIONS 3:49-51

A woman without a man cannot meet a man, any man, without thinking, even if it's for a half a second, "Perhaps this is the man."

DORIS LESSING

Single by choice. Single by design. Single through inevitable circumstances. Single via the law of averages. It doesn't really matter why you are single if you are single and unhappy about it.

I realize there are many who would say, "Better to be single than to be married and wish you weren't." But to those many, many multiplied thousands of women who await their soul mate, their Boaz, their Isaac, marriage is a desirable covenant—a prize to be treasured.

Dear sister, if this is you—if you are longing and waiting—keep moving until he has come. At some point you have to realize that companionship is not entirely about weight loss, cooking classes, makeup, self-realization, or any other tangible thing. It has something to do with timing. And just as you do not know the day nor the hour the Son of Man is coming, neither do you know when your beloved will appear in your life.

Please don't waste your precious time worrying about what you cannot control. As the Lord looks for his servants to be serving when He returns, you must keep busy attending to those things God has given you charge of. Fill your waiting time with service in the kingdom. With one hand you must work your way through depression, desperation, and despair, and with the other get busy waiting like a waitress in an exclusive restaurant. Before you know it, silent as sunlight, your prince will walk on to the pages of your life.

Just wait!

The Power of a Gift

Cast your bread upon the waters, for after many days you will find it again.

ECCLESIASTES 11:1

To have and not to give is often worse than to steal.

MARIE VON EBNER-ESCENBACH

Do you want a quick way to get someone's attention? Give a gift. There is power in gift giving. Acts of giving create—like a jackhammer thunderously stuttering through cement—passageways into wondrous places that launch us from behind the veils of our lives into new and exciting arenas.

Giving a gift or making a donation is also a two-edged sword—not only does it help the recipients meet their needs, but it blesses the giver. When you give you are making an investment into your own future. Expect a return; it is inevitable. I'm not saying the reward will be monetary. Who knows what will come of it. But by casting our bread upon the waters, we are scattering seed in a field, waiting to see what will flower and grow.

We will reap as we have sown. Remember this and be liberal in giving. It ensures a bountiful harvest. A bountiful harvest means you can easily continue the cycle that causes blessings to flow in and out of your life.

Giving good things to one another feeds us internally and we are enriched and we are satisfied. Look for ways to become involved in loving acts. As you practice the art of giving, you will become fascinated with its tremendous effect and enthralled at every opportunity to witness its power.

HΛVE YE Λ FΛTHER?

Have ye a father?

GENESIS 44:19

Fathers are still considered the most important doers in our culture, and in most families they are that . . . When fathers don't take their daughters' achievements and plans seriously, girls sometimes have trouble taking themselves seriously.

STELLA CHESS

Some of you will be able to identify with a lady I know who has a phenomenal father. He is a godly man who was always present in her childhood home, who is now an inspiration to her adult self, and who is a man whom she hopes to see traces of reflected in the image of her future mate.

Conversely, some of you may not be able to identify with the previous. For a host of reasons, some of which involve pain, many of you have never known the presence of a father or husband in the home. Many of you have had to raise children alone—and in spite of the absence of a father figure have done a beautiful job of it. We are living in an era where it is commonplace to be a single parent. Too many of you have firsthand knowledge of what it means to stand alone without the warm, strong arms of a gentle giant. Some of you may even have had circumstances in which the father or husband is indeed in the home, yet emotionally unavailable, and there is still a void left unfilled.

To you dear readers I offer the hope of the Scriptures. The Bible reminds this generation that God is a defender of the fatherless and husbandless and He is watching over you (Ps. 68:5). Take comfort in that. On the days when you feel you cannot go on—that problems big and small are sapping you of whatever strength you have—remember He is with you. Like peeling back the black face of the night sky to reveal the awe-inspiring break of day, you may delight in the intimate care and special benefits of your heavenly Father. To those of you with children, I encourage you to hold up our Lord as a perfect example of fatherhood.

This world is sometimes hard, but you are never expected to travel it alone. You have a Father and He is with you!

Family Matters

If ye then, being evil, know how to give good gifts unto your children: how much more shall your heavenly Father give the Holy Spirit to them that ask him?

LUKE 11:13 (KJV)

A family in harmony will prosper in everything.

CHINESE PROVERB

When faced with the opportunity and responsibility of building a family, please remember how important it is to give this undertaking the careful attention it requires. What you are shaping in your hands is the quality of your future, the future of your spouse and offspring. Taking the time to weave the fabric of your household into an exquisite tapestry is not a venture you will accomplish overnight. Nothing is more important than what you do with and for your families.

The first half of our lives are usually spent erroneously thinking that life is all about us, when in fact, arriving at our midway point, we suddenly begin to realize that we are here to bless and be a blessing—to help someone else through this world, not merely ourselves. This is why it is so important to think of our families.

Wherever you are in the cycle of time, it is not too late to impart something good to those persons whose lineage links with yours. If you are old, try to put into writing every ounce of wisdom and every history lesson and family story you can remember for the members of your tribe—or sit them down and relate everything to them through the age-old oral tradition. If you are midway through life's journey, provide a financial structure that will let those you leave behind pass through this world with more ease than you perhaps did. For those of you in your youth: stop, look, and listen. Be obedient enough to learn everything you can from those who go before you. The older ones have your best interests at heart in a way that those who are not of the same household do not. It is your task to glean everything from your elders so they may die empty, having passed on all they possess to you.

Whatever your situation, take up your familial responsibility. Because family matters . . . matter!

Just Do It!

He is like a tree planted by streams of water, which yields its fruit in season and whose leaf does not wither. Whatever he does prospers.

PSALM 1:3

You can't try to do things; you simply must do them.

RAY BRADBURY

For some reason, we are often more comfortable at wishful thinking than we are at actually participating in life. It is easier to think about doing something than to actually get on with it. However, as the psalmist David says, it is only what we do that will prosper.

Quite simply, effort is required on your part to do something—anything. Nothing will happen until you act. You cannot become a prayer warrior until you pray. You will not become a concert pianist until you practice daily. You cannot write by thinking about it; you must take pen and paper in hand. Nor can you heal the sick until you pray and lay hands on someone.

Action is the vehicle that accomplishes any feat. By moving in the direction of what you want, you set in motion forces to propel you into your destiny or to achieve the desired result that you long for.

So if you've been sitting around thinking about how you'd like to acquire a particular skill or accomplish a certain feat, you must make a move. Contrary to the belief that if you want something long enough, it will happen, you must put forth the effort to bring about a change in your life and circumstances. As you touch life, it will touch you back.

Bust a move, girl!

COMING IN THE ROOM

The lips of the righteous nourish many, but fools die for lack of judgment.

PROVERBS 10:21

God's answers are wiser than our prayers.

UNKNOWN

To look at the 370-pound man standing in front of me, there was nothing to make me think that the doctor would diagnose his condition as "malnourished." I remember thinking, *How can such a sizeable man suffer from malnutrition?* Think of a malnourished man and you picture a thin, waifish, and weak fellow, right? I discovered it is possible to appear outwardly healthy, yet inwardly lack the nutrients to sustain good health and a vibrant life.

It is the same in the spiritual realm. Some people waste away from emotional deprivation. Many appear to be living life well, yet inwardly suffer from a lack of love, nurturing, and the general kindnesses that lead to healthy self-esteem. If you do not feel any spiritual enthusiasm and vitality and you suspect your life is void of some things, you may be deficient and undernourished in your soul. Do not starve to death in the midst of an unseen kingdom of love. Emaciation in the soul is not necessary; it is a preventable ailment. You simply need megadoses of medicine.

There is an old song that says, "Coming in the room. Coming in the room. God's got medicine of every description coming in the room." If you know your soul is lacking, stop this very minute, reach up, and accept God's medicine. It is coming to you by way of the people God loves you through—through the messages from your pastor, your friends, and your family. You need only know you are surrounded by love and peace to receive it.

Begin to daily move in love and peace by surrounding yourself with "whatsoever things are lovely, whatsoever things are of good report" (Phil. 3:8 KJV). Enrich your soul by speaking the Word of God; feed on His presence and watch your life begin to reflect the healthiness of your soul.

Are You Down? Rejoice!

Satisfy us in the morning with your unfailing love, that we may sing for joy and be glad all our days. Make us glad for as many days as you have afflicted us, for as many years as we have seen trouble.

PSALM 90:14-15

Gloom and solemnity are entirely out of place in even the most rigorous study of an art originally intended to make glad the heart of man.

EZRA POUND

Rejoicing when you are down? Now that doesn't make much sense, does it? Or does it? Why on earth would a person rejoice when they are depressed—perhaps at their lowest point? Here is why: God in His justice controls the scales of life and it is He who corrects the inequities. The fact is you and I may go as high as we have been low. We have an opportunity to be as happy as we have been sad.

A lot of people are amazed at some of the so-called superstars.

They find it hard to understand how an Oprah Winfrey or a Maya Angelou, a T. D. Jakes, a Joe Dudley, or a coal miner's daughter can become household names and soar to unfathomed success. The answer is really quite clear if you are aware of Psalm 90. We might only notice superstars when they arrive under the soft lights of success, but most victorious people have seen dark days—the backside of the mountain. They've had their struggles the same as you and I. And look where they ended up! We need to keep that in mind. To realize that God holds remuneration for our lowest point should make us ecstatic—and relieved. It is possible to be vindicated by a divine justice system!

Many of us have been so low we easily identify with Job at "the bottom of the mountains." We have seen despair, suffered reprehensible things—and survived. But the good news is you can do more than survive. You may be given special compensation to thrive.

It is God who measures and weighs the scales of life. He balances our struggles and our trials with the ease, wholeness, and contentment required in a balanced life. Proverbs 16:11 says, "Honest scales and balances are from the Lord; all the weights in the bag are of his making." Therefore, "Cast not away . . . your confidence, which hath great recompence of reward" (Heb. 10:35).

I told you to rejoice!

Know Your Season

There is a time for everything, and a season for every activity under heaven.

ECCLESIASTES 3:1

There is a way to look at the past. Don't hide from it. It will not catch you if you don't repeat it.

PEARL BAILEY

I love to talk about raising my daughter and attending all of her school functions. I occasionally reminisce with friends about attending every PTA meeting, flag corps performance, speech contest. If it involved my Kelly, I was there.

Am I bragging? Or would I even want to be doing those same things today? A resounding no to both questions! The enthusiasm I had then was appropriate for that season of my life. I'm glad for it and proud of my daughter and happy to talk of it. But I don't need to relive it.

It's important for you to know what season of your life you're in. Then you can embrace that time and not despise those days—

they will pass like clouds moved swiftly by warm winds. The phases of your life are appointed, occurrence by occurrence, and you are only to accomplish your designated task within that specific season. If you can understand that, you will be content with each passing day of your life.

As I write to you, spring is gently nudging its soft, sweet head through the buds on the maple trees outside my door. It is not the time for me to accumulate more firewood. This is a simple analogy, but appropriate! When you can recognize a particular season of your life, you can maximize the moment for this period before entering another season, another time, another experience. Is it time to raise your children? Do it with all of your might. Are you caring for your aging parents? Do so with vigor. Perhaps you are alone. Enjoy your solitude.

No matter your age, your days are numbered and cataloged. Enjoy every delicious, precious, taxing, luscious, and perplexing moment. Like a winemaker at the press, wring the juice out of this time. You are moving on.

CALLING ALL MOTHERS!

Village life in Israel ceased, ceased until I, Deborah, arose, arose a mother in Israel.

JUDGES 5:7

What the mother sings to the cradle goes all the way to the coffin.

HENRY WARD BEECHER

After watching my daughter, Kelly, with her son, Isaac, I soon discovered a generational blessing in our family: an inherent love of motherhood. Handed down from one woman to the next in our family has been the mandate of cherishing the role of mother. Without its being preached to us or taught to us, but instead through some natural osmosis, we have innately understood the privilege and importance of parenting. It is not a responsibility we take lightly.

What I have observed in our family—that sense of nurturing—is really a privilege given to all lifegivers, whether they know and care to exercise their gift or not. We are all emotionally charged with the job of taking care of our children—of loving them, of educating them, of imparting words of light, words of healing, and words of well-being to our offspring. All of us can do this. All of us should do this. But unfortunately, all do not. And that is a tragedy whose impact will only be seen in years to come.

If you have been given the unique opportunity to form and create the life of another human being, take seriously your holy charge and get on with the business at hand. You have much work to do, with great rewards to follow. Give of yourself and your love, that you may nurture a life of love. As with all important work, what you put into this priceless task is what you will get out of it.

Little Girl, Do You See?

The Lord is my portion, saith my soul; therefore will I hope in him. The Lord is good unto them that wait for him, to the soul that seeketh him.

LAMENTATIONS 3:24-25 (KJV)

It's never too late to have a happy childhood.

TOM ROBBINS

I just reached into my closet to grab a dress to wear to work this morning and encountered my usual problem. Like most of us, I have so many beautiful clothes to choose from that many of my lovely outfits are lost in the midst of abundance. So much stuff!

Am I bragging? Of course not! In actuality, most of my clothes are gifts. What I am, however, is amazed!

There is a little girl I knew very well forty or so years ago who would have been amazed to know that in her future she would have a choice between scores of lovely outfits to wear each day. I know that little girl would have stood wide-eyed and open-mouthed in disbelief—and shouting with glee—to think that some of the things she had daydreamed about and wanted were really going to happen.

All too often, when we become adults we forget our childhood dreams and prayers and what we wanted very badly for ourselves when we grew up. We had so many things we wished for and knew were impossible to have. Dreams of ballerinas or astronauts, movie stars or cowboys. Dreams of family or wealth or exotic locales. We willed with all our might to have them become reality. Yet somewhere in the midst of the passing years, we slowly lost touch with those dreams. We closed the diaries and locked away the scrapbooks and gave away the toys and instead took up the reins of the "real world"—work and deadlines and paychecks and bills.

I urge you to once again look back at your childhood dreams and hopes. Have you accomplished any of them? Can you? It's important to remember where you came from, and if you can reclaim even the tiniest, most minute thing, then do so—and remember that everything you have or will ever have comes from the faithful, loving, and almighty hand of God.

Come, little girl. What are you waiting for?

Everyone Has One!

Wherefore he saith, When he ascended up on high, he led captivity captive, and gave gifts unto men.

Ephesians 4:8 (KJV)

Talent is like electricity. We don't understand electricity. We use it.

Maya Angelou

Have you ever wondered what your gift or talent is? You can be sure that you do indeed have one. Whether you have discovered it or whether it is yet hiding unobserved, it is there. I repeat: you have a gift.

Gifts are mysterious presents hidden within us, waiting to be discovered. Most of us use our gifts without noticing it, only to one day realize that our method of handling a particular situation so easily was actually a treasure that was specially given to us. I remember my mother commenting often to me that she wished she could type. I thought it a silly statement at the time; surely anyone and everyone could perform such a simple task. I later realized that what I had placed so little value on was one of my gifts. Because I had not esteemed what I could do easily I had almost not recognized that I had been endowed with a tool that would one day provide for my needs—as a writer and editor, I make my living through my fingertips.

The person who types as fast as she can talk should realize that a gift has been placed in her hands. The one who speaks eloquently and easily in front of crowds must recognize the power of her ability to communicate. The woman who cannot remember being unable to sing or play music needs to remember that not everyone can do so. The person who has the gift of being able to teach others must take advantage of it and give others the benefit of her learning.

I remember a lady in our neighborhood who had the cleanest house I have ever seen. Every article and piece of paper was in place. Night or day, her home was in impeccable order. Unaware of her abilities, she was a recipient of welfare. She would have made someone an incredible office assistant, and with a few classes, a great administrative assistant. Her organizational abilities came naturally to her. In fact, she thrived on providing order. Yet she never capitalized on her gift, because she never appreciated it.

Are you one of these people? Or are you perhaps one of the others whose gifts lie dormant within and must be explored, developed, and cultivated? Look closely. What keepsake has God given you that you have yet to discover and acknowledge and use? Seek it out and make it yours!

BIG THINGS MOVE SLOWLY

*For the vision is yet for an appointed time, but at the end it
shall speak, and not lie: though it tarry, wait for it; because it
will surely come, it will not tarry.*

HABBAKKUK 2:3 (KJV)

Patience is a necessary ingredient of genius.

BENJAMIN DISRAELI

A lot of people maneuver through life nestled down in the bed
of complacency, dragging through a slow-motion life as if
drugged, lulled by the tune of boredom and calmly submitting to
defeat. But you don't belong to that crowd—if you have a dream.

Do you have a dream? I hope so. Dreamers are inspired to go
farther than they have ever gone before and encouraged to
become more than what they had previously contemplated.
Dreamers have a fervency and zeal that is contagious.

But there is a challenge to your dreamer's enthusiasm and
excitement. If God has placed a very large vision within your
heart, you will have to develop the ability to see your gleaming

future . . . and yet wait for its manifestation. You may spend many years like Moses on the backside of a mountain being prepared to fulfill your dream. You may spend many years in prison like Joseph, delayed but not denied while you anticipate your vision. Even Esther took a full year to prepare to see her king.

Your having the faith to wait on your time is the strength of your dream. The longer you wait, the bigger the dream. The bigger your dream, the more glorious the outcome.

If what God has promised you has been a very long time coming, get ready. You are going to experience a blessing of enormous proportion!

Book Learning

The heart of the wise teacheth his mouth, and addeth learning to his lips.

PROVERBS 16:23

When I stand before God at the end of my life, I would hope that I would not have a single bit of talent left, and could say, "I used everything you gave me."

ERMA BOMBECK

I don't know which of the teachings my mother imparted to her children would be deemed the best present—there were so many! Of one thing, however, I am sure: my love of reading is a gift that I am most thankful for.

Mother made sure of our education. My brothers and I could read before entering first grade. We had a library card that was used often. Many Saturdays were spent lounging about the house reading or exploring the library shelves for that perfect story. What a treasure to have had such an upbringing. And it is one that has followed me through the years.

Today, to sit curled up in a big, soft chair, coffee close by, good book in hand—or to lay curled up in bed with the covers wrapped around my neck and the soothing tones of an audio book absorbing me into another time and place—is better than three scoops of Calgon in a bath of steamy, hot water. Reading is sunshine to the soul. Emotionally I am transported to another dimension. I have a reprieve from whatever is going on in my life and am restored to unwrap another day.

You too have the ability to make the great escape to wherever you would like to be. Make the choice to spend more time with a book. Promise yourself that you will more often stop and read a few passages from good writing. If you have family, encourage them as well. Set aside a half hour each evening for family book time and take turns reading to each other. You will soon find yourself looking forward to those precious moments together where you can experience other places and things.

Reading is inspiration enough to put a smile on your face and pep in your step and to renew your hope to just keep moving. What are you waiting for? Turn the page. Read on!

LIGHT THE DARK

And God saw the light, that it was good: and God divided the light from the darkness.

GENESIS 1:4 (KJV)

Light is not recognized except through darkness.

JEWISH PROVERB

Have you ever watched joggers at night? Those without reflecting lights on their shoes or light-colored shirts seem to think we can see them. But as you know, we can't, until we are right upon them. I understand, though, why some think they can be seen in the dark. Many probably feel their inner illumination shines outward; they think others can see what they sense about their inner selves. And so they are confident.

So it needs to be with us. God gives us one another to light the darkness. What you and I must seek to do is uncover the light we possess—the light that is hidden within us—and let it shine through our good works and friendly disposition so others may truly see us. Let us daily strive to let the risen Savior flow through us and outward to our fellow man. After all, like stars that light the night, we are His sunbeams in this earthly realm.

Unveiling our light is a process. Jesus said, "Is a candle brought to be put under a bushel?" (Matt. 4:21 KJV). He was telling us to shine bright. Our way to shine is through our good works. It is through our deeds that we are unveiled and revealed. When you help someone in need, you are lighting the dark.

Recently, a member of our church's hospital committee spoke of contacting a parishioner who had become very ill. Upon placing the call and speaking with the wife of the stricken man, our volunteer became amazed at the woman's gratefulness. She was amazed to receive calls and caring during a low point in their lives. To the recipient of the call, light had flooded a dark area for them. They were better able to cope after this deed of kindness.

The axiom "Action speaks louder than words" is true. Test the power of good deeds by performing something for someone who needs assistance. The recipient's warm response is going to be the sign that lets you know your candle is burning brightly and that you have brought illumination into her life.

Find your light. Let it shine.

The Only Thing about a Risk Is Not Taking One

Now there were four men with leprosy at the entrance of the city gate. They said to each other, "Why stay here until we die? If we say, 'We'll go into the city'—the famine is there, and we will die. And if we stay here, we will die. So let's go over to the camp of the Arameans and surrender. If they spare us, we live; if they kill us, then we die."

2 KINGS 7:3-4

Anything I've ever done that ultimately was worthwhile . . . initially scared me to death.

BETTY BENDER

In the time it takes to blink an eye, life can change from disastrous to wondrous. From mundane to exhilarating, bordering on sensory overload. From a dry valley to a flood-level stage. When we are offered an opportunity to initiate radical change rather than allow ourselves to be helplessly sucked into a funnel of unfamiliar circumstances, we feel more in control.

But what of those who are unwilling, unable, or too afraid to answer a call into the unknown?

Do you remember the story of the four leprous men who sat starving outside the city gate? They took a risk. "Why stay here until we die?" they said. Off they went into the city and were blessed to eat and drink and receive supplies. Had they not taken that risk they would have starved to death within walking distance of abundance.

What blessing are you within walking distance of? Do you have an enticing and sound opportunity to move to another city, to enter into a promising relationship, to do something you have never done before? Or to do something you have never seen done before? It will require your taking a risk.

For each of us there comes a time to make a decision to do the extraordinary, the challenging, the unique. Worse than any failure or botched attempt is the horror of looking back at the gloomy cloak of regret that will hang down around your knees like an old garment that has lost its elasticity. Is that what you want?

Nothing ventured, nothing gained. What if?

Stop It!

Therefore I tell you, do not worry about your life, what you will eat; or about your body, what you will wear. Life is more than food, and the body more than clothes.

LUKE 12:22-23

Courage is the price that life extracts for granting peace. The soul that knows it not, knows no release from little things, knows not the livid loneliness of fear.

AMELIA EARHART

Yes, I said "Stop it!" That's the best way for me to tell you about handling worrying. Simply refuse to allow this destructive behavior into your life.

As a former chronic worrier, I am practicing more and more the art of casting my fate to the wind. Actually, I have seen God do too many incredible and magnificent things in my life to continue to dwell on things I can't control anyway. It is rather insulting to the Creator to respond to His kindness and faithfulness with worry.

Recently, I was on the Internet during a huge storm. As you probably know, in Texas storms can be a life-threatening situation, and this particular storm did a lot of damage not too far from where I live. But because I had only casually heard about the storm, I did not track the news reports and decided to continue with the project I was working on. I didn't worry about what was happening around me. Later I heard about the damage.

Would it have done me any good to worry during the storm? No.

We must stop the cycle of worry. It is a disservice to ourselves to alarm our spirit, disturb our peace, and carry heavy burdens that are best left in the lap of the Lord. Worry is a self-inflicted wound and a learned habit that causes great personal suffering. Not only can you erase this unnecessary pattern, you can reverse it. How? Let go of the temptation to become negatively involved. Release every false effort to control the uncontrollable. Engage God in your affairs like a little child who sees her parents coming to her aid and realizes she has no need to worry.

The next time a situation arises in your life that seemingly requires worry, simply refuse to participate in overly concerning yourself with whatever is going on. Soon you will notice that uneasiness gives way to calm and anxiety slips from you like a silk camisole off weary shoulders.

Feel like worrying? Stop it!

You've Got to Really, Really Want Out

When Jesus saw him lying there and learned that he had been in this condition for a long time, he asked him, "Do you want to get well?"

JOHN 5:6

Do not pray for easy lives. Pray to be stronger men. Do not pray for tasks equal to your powers. Pray for power equal to your tasks.

PHILLIPS BROOKS

"Do you want to get well?" That seems like a silly question for Jesus to ask a man who had been ill for a great length of time. But you would be amazed at the people who "use" their sickness for various reasons and who don't want their condition to change.

Be careful that you don't use your medical condition as a crutch. I would not dare insult you and say you're doing so. But as someone who has come through a debilitating illness, I would seek to enlighten, expose, and challenge you. During my long recovery, I daily checked on every level, behind every nook and cranny in my mental, physical, emotional, and spiritual life, to see what might prevent me from getting better. That is the reason I bring this issue to your attention.

Jesus too knew that not everyone wants to get well; He would not have otherwise asked such a seemingly ridiculous question. For those of you who haven't suffered an illness, it's more deceptive than you think. After days or weeks or years, it sometimes becomes second nature to feel the way you do and to believe in it.

Don't let any little trick of the enemy seduce you into staying in an undesirable set of circumstances a nanosecond longer than necessary. A need for attention or control or sympathy, a feeling of hopelessness, and a host of other reasons may be at work against you. If so, remember that you can and should get through it. You must let nothing separate you from the love of God and the healing, delivering power that is part of His care.

Kingdom Against Kingdom: Sassy Survivors

Nation will rise against nation, and kingdom against kingdom.

MATTHEW 24:7

What lies behind us and what lies before us are tiny matters compared to what lies within us.

RALPH WALDO EMERSON

Women as warriors! Oh, my! What an unpleasant topic to include in a women's devotional. Or is it? Mixed in between these pages of grace, beauty, and tenderness, we have another element of life to consider. How to fight. And when to fight. And what to fight.

I advise you to arm yourselves with weapons of mass destruction. (I heard you gasp.) These, however, won't be the weapons of this world (e.g., 9-millimeters, Uzis, tankers, and other tools of annihilation). Your weapons are less cumbersome to operate . . . and mightier. You will utilize the weapons of faith. You must use your faith, which works by love, to demolish every stronghold that exalts itself against the knowledge of God. You must capture all negative and evil thoughts and bring them into obedience to the laws of Christ's kingdom.

Perhaps you think your weapons aren't threatening enough for what you face. No so. The Scriptures tell us that by faith kingdoms were conquered, promises were gained, the mouths of lions were shut, flames were quenched, escapes were made, and weaknesses were turned to strengths. Even if you face a conflict that wasn't listed above, be confident—you may use the force of your own faith, the enthusiasm and insight from the Spirit, and the knowledge from the Word of God to obtain anything else needed to overcome your opposition.

Today more than ever, with Americans having faced a physical attack upon this nation, we must use the force of our faith to overcome the threats and actions of our enemies. It will be our faith in God and our trust in His covering and protection that provide the weapons to destroy our foe. From your bedrooms, your cars, and your kitchens, you can pray in faith, believing in God for victory as we wage war against this present darkness. There is no force stronger than love, and faith works by love. Use it.

Ready! Aim! Fire!!!

GETTING UNSTUCK

*And she besought him that he would cast forth the devil out of
her daughter. But Jesus said unto her, Let the children first be
filled: for it is not meet to take the children's bread, and to cast
it unto the dogs. And she answered and said unto him, Yes,
Lord: yet the dogs under the table eat of the children's crumbs.
And he said unto her, For this saying go thy way; the devil is
gone out of thy daughter.*

MARK 7:26-29 (KJV)

*If you always do what you've always done, you'll always get
what you have always gotten.*

UNKNOWN

For some reason, many Christians operate in the valley of inde-
cision, supposing that their religion, their walk with Christ,
requires no input and has no obligation. These people belong to
the silent majority. But Christianity is a speaking faith—a faith
that involves action. You must say something. You must do something to be effective in Christ's kingdom.

To provoke change, our mode of operation must change.

It takes a dedicated handmaiden of the Lord to be sensitive to the Spirit and to recognize that her waiting period is over. Like a doctor who induces labor because it's time for the baby to be born lest a beautiful event become life-threatening, you must take it upon yourself to act. Remember the woman with the issue of blood who touched the hem of Jesus' garment, a practice forbidden in her day but one that netted her phenomenal results. Or do as the woman whose daughter was ill. She too broke with tradition and order and began to worship Jesus. And because of this—because she took an active role—her daughter was saved.

Sometimes we have to go against the grain to get what we want. Getting unstuck requires acts of faith. Not just standing in faith, not even just praying in faith, but moving in faith.

TIME OUT FOR TIME-OUT!

Blessed is the man whom God corrects; so do not despise the discipline of the Almighty.

JOB 5:17

I do not feel obliged to believe that the same God who has endowed us with sense, reason, and intellect has intended us to forgo their use.

GALILEO GALILEI

Despite the propaganda you hear in news, the subtle persuasion of Hollywood, and the teachings of today, dare to discipline your child.

Because the Word of God is not the guiding light of this secular world, many no longer heed the truth of Scriptures. But even without the Word of God, one should be able to see the difference in the life of a child who has had structure, discipline, and loving correction. Conversely, you don't have to be a rocket scientist to see that those things that are not corrected and repaired ultimately come to ruin.

I am all for sitting little Johnny and cute Susie in the corner when they have misbehaved. I believe in communication with children to make sure they are understood and emotionally okay and to make sure they can understand and follow instructions. Time-out is great when it works. *If* it works. But, if little Johnny and cute Susie continually wreak havoc wherever they appear and don't respect the message of the chair-in-the-corner scenario, then a "trip to the shed" will work wonders.

My position affords me the opportunity to speak with many felons and prison inmates. Most of them say the same thing: had they been provided a disciplined life, they would not be behind bars. Of course, sometimes even a well-raised child takes the wrong path and ends up regretting it. But those who end up in prison despite good parenting are easier to rehabilitate and less likely to become repeat offenders.

My mother often said to her children, "I am going to discipline you so that the policeman doesn't, so that the gangs won't, and so that the world will have a better and more productive citizen." Set parameters for your children and discipline them with love if they cross those boundaries.

It's time-out time for nonproductive techniques that do not work.

It Takes a Village

If a house is divided against itself, that house cannot stand.

MARK 3:25

If one is out of touch with oneself, then one cannot touch others.

ANNE MORROW LINDBERGH

There is an African proverb that says, "It takes a village to raise a child." Hillary Clinton made this quote popular a few years ago. I agree completely—I think it takes a village to do almost anything in this world. There is an element of safety in numbers. More arms to reach, more eyes to see, more ears to hear. There is obvious strength in unity.

When my own family—a village—came together as a unit during our mother's illness, we were a united force. In what was to be mere seconds before my mother left this earth, it was my daughter Kelly, Mother's first grandchild, who, having a premedical background from college studies, happened to glance at the monitors and read the instruments to realize that Momma was leaving this earthly realm. She alerted us to come from the adjacent room to gather around her bed and bid her farewell. We were all in place because of her skills, sharp eye, and quick actions. Everyone has a part to play in this life.

Family, friends, and relationships are important. We can never devalue the role we will play in each other's lives, and it is important that we take each other seriously. We must respectfully and lovingly consider one another as valuable gems.

You Can't Hear God If You're Screaming!

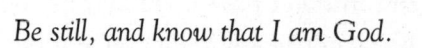

Be still, and know that I am God.

PSALM 46:10

Silence is precious, for it is of God. In silence all God's acts are done; in silence alone can his voice be heard and his word spoken.

SISTER JANET

There is so much to be said for operating in the silence of God. "Quiet power," a lady in my office called it. Through silence we are able to enter into the quiet and magnificent presence of God.

God is never really apart from us. It is not that He lives in one dimension and we in another. God is omnipresent; He is everywhere. Irrespective of how we neglect and ignore Him when we are busy with our daily work and preoccupied with our own lives, He is there. We need only reach out to touch Him, to whisper or think His name. His presence overwhelms us. We can sense His reality with our spirit.

Perhaps you are more the type who reaches out to the Lord in exultation and shouts of glory. But remember, our salvation is not predicated upon who screams or quickens the loudest and with the greatest appearance of anointing. Many women are like Mary, the sister of Martha, who sat quietly at the feet of Jesus, listening, being taught words of life (Luke 10:39).

So I challenge you: if you have not learned to listen for God through blessed silence, then you must surely give it a try. Practice connecting with Him in quiet power. He may be trying to tell you something, and you can't hear God if you're too busy screaming!

I Believe I Can Fly

Whoever would be great among you must be your servant.

MARK 10:43

Service is the rent you pay for the space you occupy on the earth.

SHIRLEY CHISHOLM

Don't you love a winner? I do. People like Tiger Woods, Serena and Venus Williams, Princess Diana, Hank Aaron, Oprah, and Mother Teresa make our spirit soar. But what is the driving force behind achievers? What is the wind in their sails that causes them to fly before all others?

I believe it is the wind of adversity that moves many people supernaturally to high ground. The very thing that seemingly would hinder them causes peak performers to excel. Their place of brokenness incites them to succeed against the odds.

Is your life in a low state? Yet do you yearn for greatness? Remember: Jesus takes the foolishness of this world to confound the wise; He uses weakness to show off His strength and He ushers those at the back of the line to the front. If you are the least likely to succeed and you are willing to serve, like the leavening in a batch of mouthwatering, homemade rolls, keep serving. You will rise to the top.

People who serve carry a spirit of humility. You cannot care for, wait upon, or tend to others with a prideful spirit. We are told in the Scriptures that if we humble ourselves under the mighty hand of God, He will exalt us in due time (1 Pet. 5:6-10). Recognizing the hand of God, then, is of utmost importance. You may need to look closely at what is occurring in your life to make the appropriate response.

God has a way of exalting the little-known, unsung people and making their names great. Remember Abraham? But it really should come as no surprise whom God selects—just look for the humble servants among you. They are already in motion and ready to take flight.

Afterword

Writing *Sister Wit* has been an enlightening, exhilarating, and yes, exhausting experience. I wrote the entire book on my laptop from a black kitchen stool in my den/study. The stool used to be red and white, and the old paint is showing through all the chips and dings. To my daughter's horror, I have kept this little stool through the years. To me it is a reminder of our early days of deprivation, struggle, and just plain hard days—days of trusting God and waiting and watching Him deliver me and my daughter and bring us through whatever battles we faced. This little kitchen stool is a memorial of my life.

I am constantly amazed at the strategy and the greatness of God. His ways are beyond our thinking, beyond our finding out. What exactly do I mean? It is this. I had no intention of writing a book. I was quite content to write romantic poetry for myself and articles for my place of employment. I had no aspirations of sharing my thoughts, my inside places, with women of God worldwide. You see, I am a private individual. I had not even shared the details of my surgery with anyone. Ever. It was my brother, Bishop Jakes, who urged me to write my testimony. I was actually horrified at the suggestion. Who would want to know about what I had gone through? What would make him think I would ever want to revisit that place? What gall to ask me to share the darkest period of my life with people I did not and would never know!

You know what I'm about to say to you, don't you? What I received from writing *Sister Wit* brought healing into my heart and soul. I was confronted with the task of writing words my lips had never uttered. For twenty years I had told no one of the horror of what I had gone through. For twenty years I had not spoken of the physical and mental anguish that tortured me in those days. *Sister Wit* forced me to acknowledge verbally what I had only lived out in my head.

Certainly I wrote this book for you, but in writing to you, I received a release, a refreshening. Strength. I had no idea the restoration in store for me. My goal was to give to you words that I personally knew would strengthen, guide, enlighten, and applaud you on life's perplexing, sometimes arduous, journey. My motive in *Sister Wit* was to let you know that you can go to hell emotionally and come back—that you can survive the greatest storm and the blackest night. I know.

It is my sincere hope that this book blesses you as it has me. What a delight it has been to me to pick up the pages of this manuscript and read a few lines and find that I am blessed by what I've written to you. I hope I have ministered to you as I have to myself.

I sought to speak to all women in this book. I think there is something on these pages for every lady. But my heart's desire is to talk with women who have lost hope. I rose in the middle of the night to write this piece, not because I am depressed or distraught, but because I have been thinking of a particular segment of society—those of you who feel you have reached the end of your strength. I write to you women who feel you are unable even to turn the pages of this book, who don't have the strength to bring a spoon to your lips during mealtime, who cannot walk outside and get into a car and go for a ride, who cannot form your next thought with clarity, who have not been hugged in such a long time you cannot remember what a soft, warm touch feels like, and who have had illnesses of such catastrophic proportions that for someone to even think of encouraging you seems a preposterous and ridiculous idea.

I write you to remind you there exists a mighty God who does unthinkable, unimaginable, and utterly impossible things like walk on water and raise stinking-dead people from the grave and bring people out of comas and turn the world upside down to deliver and make whole people just like you.

I encourage you. God ushered me from my bed tonight to remind you that He is mindful of you. You are not forgotten in your dark night. He is with you. He is where medicine cannot reach. He is where sound cannot travel and where darkness is the deepest and where pain is the most extreme. And although your plight may seem an absolutely hopeless situation, with God all things are possible. Even now. May hope, which is the anchor for your soul, spring forth to pull your falling soul to safety and total well-being.

And may God be with you and me today, even as we face never-before-seen challenges. America is at war. Am I shocked?

No. I am filled with righteous indignation at what has taken place on our soil, but I am not mesmerized by the enemy's efforts to steal our peace. I am not astonished at the fragility of life. Once you have personally encountered and become an eyewitness to tragedy within your own soul, body, and mind, you are never again shocked beyond reason at the frailness of our existence. But I am reminded of Psalm 27, which begins, "The Lord is my light and my salvation." Now more than ever, every believer must rise above the death, destruction, fear, and turmoil that seeks to fixate our gaze upon its snare. You and I, sister, must continue doing the things Christ would have us do. Love one another. And remember, "In order for evil to continue, good men must do nothing." Do those things that bless and do not curse. What we do with and to one another will make a difference in the quality of our lives. I pray this book is a beam of light that you may escape upon during any trial or other disturbances this nation may face.

Sister Wit is written to be read often. It is a book to be kept near your bed, in your office, wherever you may rest so you may randomly pick it up and find a nugget, a revelation, some direction for your life. In *Sister Wit* I have shared with you my life, my pain, my triumphs, and my God. May at least one thing I have written here give you peace and joy.

Jacqueline Jakes
Dallas, Texas